A Close Shave

Champignol Malgré Lui

Georges Feydeau
in collaboration with Maurice Desvallières
Translated by Peter Meyer

Published by the British Broadcasting Corporation,
35 Marylebone High Street, London W1M 4AA
ISBN 0 563 12594 2
First published 1974

Printed in England by Tonbridge Printers Ltd

Translator's Note

This translation was commissioned by the BBC for broadcasting, but I have here ignored my radio adaptation and reverted to the original text. Feydeau's stage directions frequently include the relative positions of the characters, which are numbered from left to right, so that, for example, 1 is always left of 2 but may be anywhere on the stage.

The Italian uncle, Romeo, has been changed from a Swiss, Chamel, to provide jokes about his name and because references to the absence of military service in Switzerland and the prevalence of Swiss porters in Paris would now be unintelligible. I have assumed that he and his family would use the Italian pronunciation of Romeo, but that Saint Florimond in his ignorance would pronounce it in the usual English fashion. In Act II I have made all the recruits Reservists, instead of some of them being Territorials, and for the drill sequences I have adopted the simplifications and clarifications used by Stuart Burge in his production at the Nottingham Playhouse, including the elimination of two additional squads of recruits with their attendant corporals.

This translation was first broadcast on 27 December 1968 with the following cast:

Saint Florimond	*Richard Briers*
Angele	*Gwen Watford*
Joseph	*John Baddeley*
Charlotte	*Rosalind Shanks*
Romeo	*Andre van Gyseghem*
Mauricette	*Pamela Miles*
Dufoulay	*Michael Spice*
Capt Camaret	*Simon Lack*
Adrienne	*Helen Weir*
Celestin	*Graham Armitage*
Police Sergeant	*John Pullen*
Champignol	*John Moffatt*
Lt Ledoux	*Fraser Kerr*
Sgt Belouette	*Frederick Treves*
Lafauchette	*Antony Viccars*
Prince of Valence	*John Humphry*
Major Fourrageot	*Peter Pratt*
Corporal Grosbon	*Victor Lucas*
Barber	*John Baddeley*
Jerome	*David Brierly*

Produced by John Tydeman

The first stage production was at the Nottingham Playhouse on 10 July 1971 with the following cast:

Saint Florimond	*Jimmy Thompson*
Angele	*Angela Richards*
Joseph	*Geoffrey Drew*
Charlotte	*Susan Littler*
Romeo	*Paul Dawkins*
Mauricette	*Delia Lindsay*
Dufoulay	*Neil Fitzwilliam*
Capt Camaret	*David Dodimead*
Adrienne	*Gail Harrison*
Celestin	*Simon Cadell*
Police Sergeant	*Martin Matthews*
Policeman	*Melvyn Hastings*
Champignol	*Donald Gee*
Lt Ledoux	*Michael Elphick*
Sgt Belouette	*Peter Childs*
Lafauchette	*David Schofield*
Prince of Valence	*Charles Waite*
Lavalanche	*Hywel Davies*
Badin	*Peter Ellis*
Major Fourrageot	*Martin Matthews*
Corporal Grosbon	*Melvyn Hastings*
A Barber	*Geoffrey Drew*
Jerome	*Peter Ellis*
Reservists	*Michael Barnard*
	Michael Barry
	Kevin Cole
	Paul Greenwood
	Timothy Seward
	Harry Stephenson

Directed by Stuart Burge
Settings by Patrick Robertson
Costumes by Rosemary Vercoe

Characters
In Order of Appearance

SAINT FLORIMOND	
ANGELE	*Champignol's wife*
JOSEPH	*Her manservant*
CHARLOTTE	*Her maid*
ROMEO	*Her uncle*
MAURICETTE	*Romeo's daughter*
DUFOULAY	*Her husband*
CAPT. CAMARET	
ADRIENNE	*His daughter*
CELESTIN	*His nephew*
POLICE SERGEANT	
CHAMPIGNOL	
LT LEDOUX	
SGT BELOUETTE	*Reservists*
LAFAUCHETTE	*Reservists*
PRINCE OF VALENCE	*Reservists*
LAVALANCHE	*Reservists*
BADIN	*Reservists*
MAJOR FOURRAGEOT	
CORPORAL GROSBON	
A BARBER	
JEROME	*A manservant*
A POLICEMAN	
SIX RESERVISTS	

ACT I The Champignols' flat in Paris
ACT II The Barracks at Clermont. The next day
ACT III Mme Rivolet's House in Clermont. The same evening
The time is about 1890

Act I

(The Champignols' flat in Paris. On the right is the door of Angele's bedroom. On the left, downstage, a door leading to the rest of the flat. Midstage a big window, and in the back wall a door opening into the hall. At the back of the hall is the front door of the flat.
Pictures on easels, sketches on the walls etc. On the right, downstage, is a table, with a chair on each side of it. On the table a cup of chocolate on a tray. On the left a sofa with two upright chairs on its right. Against the back wall on a chair is a canvas with its back to the audience.
When the curtain rises, the stage is empty. A cuckoo clock strikes eight, then a key can be heard in the front door which opens.
Saint Florimond enters)

St Florimond (*Coming downstage centre*) Phew! I'm here. Oh, it's so silly! My heart's going bang, bang, bang! I can hear it. Oh, if you've anything wrong with your tonsils, don't ever risk a love affaire. (*He goes upstage*) If I were her husband, I'd come in here, calm and collected. But I'm not . . . Ah, well, be brave.

(*He goes behind the right-hand table to the door and knocks on it*)

Angele (*Off*) Is that you, Victoire?

St Florimond (*Woman's voice*) Yes. . . . (*Aside*) She'll be furious.

Angele (*Off*) Come in then.

St Florimond (*As before*) Yes.

(*He opens the door*)

Angele (*Off. Screaming*) Oh! You! . . . Go away.

St Florimond Oh! She's getting out of the bath.

Angele (*Off*) Shut the door. Shut the door.

St Florimond Yes, no . . . Well . . . (*The door slams in his face*) Oh!

What did I say? She'd be furious. What did I say? Women are funny. (*He sits*) If I were her husband . . I'd come in here . . . calm and collected . . . I'm her lover . . . So I'm kicked out. That's life. When I think I've been cooling my heels for two hours outside on the pavement! (*He sits at the table, right, with his back to Angele's door*) Oh, no! My heart! . . . There are two things that upset me. Excitement. And hunger. I've had no breakfast this morning. (*He sees the cup of chocolate and drinks it as he goes on talking*) . . . And heaven knows when I'll get any. But, pah! Lovers don't need food. (*He swallows the rest of the chocolate*)

(*Angele enters right and stands facing the audience at the end of the table at which Saint Florimond is sitting*)

Angele What is the meaning of this behaviour?

St Florimond Angele, I will only say one word. (*Stuffing a piece of toast in his mouth and talking with his mouth full*) It's love.

Angele (*Coming downstage*) For heaven's sake! You've been drinking my chocolate!

St Florimond Your chocolate? It is good!

Angele *Is* good?

St Florimond Hm. Was good.

Angele Really, this is outrageous! I forbid you to set foot in this house again and here you are at eight in the morning!

St Florimond I didn't want to compromise you.

Angele Pah! . . . Anyway someone must have seen you.

(*Saint Florimond rises and goes to the door into the hall to make sure no one's coming, then he comes back downstage next to Angele*)

St Florimond No, they didn't. I thought . . . this is the moment . . . the moment when the servants go out . . . every day. So I waited till they'd gone. Besides I knew your husband had been away for the past month. So I thought: she's alone!

Angele I told you not to come. I wrote to you, didn't I? 'Everything is finished between us. Send me back my key. The key I so foolishly gave you.'

St Florimond It's because of the key I'm here. . . . Hm, that's how I got in.

Angele (*Moving to the extreme left, level with the sofa*) You didn't have to *come*! You could have posted it.

St Florimond (*Following her*) I thought of that. But apparently you have to write on the parcel what's in it . . . Well, I couldn't put 'Madame Champignol's front-door key'. What would the man in the post office think?

Angele (*Sitting on the sofa*) You don't have to say everything.

St Florimond (*Standing next to her*) Besides . . . I did have another reason for coming here. I thought: No, the last word has not been said. That farewell letter can't be final. Or it wouldn't have filled me with hope.

Angele Hope? What filled you with hope?

St Florimond 'Everything is finished between us.'

Angele That filled you with hope?

St Florimond Of course. Everything can't possibly be finished, I thought, because nothing ever started. . . So if she begins with the end, perhaps she'll end with the beginning. (*He sits on the sofa at 2, next to Angele*)

Angele (*Mockingly*) Oh! Oh!

St Florimond Angele! (*He tries to seize her by the waist*)

Angele (*Releasing herself, rising and moving to 2*) No! No more Angele, my dear! Thank you very much. No more little escapades!

St Florimond (*Rising and following her*) What escapades?

Angele Well! Like Fontainebleau!

St Florimond (*At 1*) That was a disaster.

Angele (*At 2*) It was virtue triumphant.

St Florimond That wasn't your fault.

Angele (*Sitting on the chair at the left of the right-hand table*) You think so?

St Florimond (*Passing behind the table, then coming downstage on the other side*) I don't suppose you agreed to spend two days with me at Fontainebleau to look at the palace (*Sitting on the chair on the other side of the table, facing Angele*) If you hadn't run into those relations of yours from the country . . . your uncle . . . What's his name?

Angele Romeo.

St Florimond A splendid name for an uncle!

Angele He's Italian.

St Florimond If you hadn't run into your Uncle Romeo, his daughter and her husband . . .

Angele (*Rising and moving to the left at 1*) Yes. What about that? It was typical of you.

(*Saint Florimond rises and comes downstage towards her*)

There are hundreds of other towns in France besides Fontainebleau. Dozens of other hotels besides the Golden Lion. But you have to pick the one hotel in the one town that they choose for their honeymoon.

St Florimond How could I know?

Angele You should have found out.

St Florimond (*At 2*) All right! Next time I go to a hotel, I'll ask if they've any Romeos about the place!

Angele (*At 1*) Look what happened! They think you're my husband.

St Florimond You didn't have to tell them.

Angele I didn't tell them. . . . Not knowing my husband and seeing you alone with me at Fontainebleau, of course they thought . . .

St Florimond That I was Champignol. And as your husband's a painter, your uncle kept on pestering me to do a sketch for him. I did him a 'Mountain Peak', all on my own. Oh, I won't forget Fontainebleau.

Angele (*Moving to 2*) Nor will I. Thank heavens they never come to Paris! Anyway, I've decided not to proceed any further. Give me back my key.

t Florimond (*At 1*) Give me back my key! You really mean you want it to end like this . . . just fizzle out?

Angele Yes.

t Florimond But that's dishonest. You made me believe you were in love with me.

Angele I know. You see, you arrived at the psychological moment. My husband was away, I met you at a party, you pursued me . . .

t Florimond You fell in love with me.

Angele No, I was bored . . . Perhaps I did believe I was in love with you. But as Heaven decreed I should emerge unscathed, I'm now going to be faithful to my husband. He's charming, intelligent; it's not as if he were . . .

(*Clock strikes the half-hour: 'Cuckoo'*)

I beg your pardon?

t Florimond (*Midstage at 1*) It wasn't me . . . It was the clock.

Angele (*Extreme right*) I should hope so!

t Florimond (*Going towards her*) You know, you're right. It's never worth while trying to patch up a love affaire. This one's a failure, on to the next!

Angele Now you're being sensible. If I were to give you a word of advice, it would be to give up all these affaires of yours. And get married.

St Florimond (*Indignant*) Get married! (*Changing*) I'm just going to.

Angele Just going to! . . . You never mentioned it.

St Florimond I was afraid it would annoy you.

Angele (*Going upstage to 2*) How thoughtful! And who are you thinking of marrying? (*Sitting on a chair to the left of the table*)

St Florimond (*Standing next to her at 1*) I don't know. A girl I'm due to meet tomorrow night at a ball her aunt's giving. A Madame Rivolet; I hardly even know *her*

Angele Where is this ball?

St Florimond At Clermont, a little town in Brittany.

Angele Oh! That's a long way. Is the girl pretty?

St Florimond Is she pretty! Sixty thousand francs a year!

Angele (*Rising and moving to 1*) Oh! Well, you mustn't heistate. Go right ahead!

St Florimond That was my intention.

Angele I'd never have believed it. . . After the propositions you've just made to me!

St Florimond (*At 1*) That! . . . That was for now! . . . But, well, you're right. If we have to part, let's part.

Angele Exactly. Now you must go. If the servants come back . . .

(*They go upstage to the hall door. Voices can be heard*)

Heavens! Here they are!

St Florimond How can I get out? (*He hurries towards the room on the right, passing behind the table*)

Angele No, not that way! That's my bedroom!

St Florimond Too bad!

(*Saint Florimond goes out into Angele's room. Joseph enters from the hall*)

Angele What is it, Joseph?

Joseph (*Upstage, left of the hall door at 1*) I've just done the shopping.

Angele (*Behind the table, at 2*) I don't care what you've done. What do you want?

Joseph Didn't you find my message last night?

Angele (*Coming downstage, as does Joseph*) Message?

Joseph Yes. As you were late, I left a message on the table next to your bed . . . (*Suddenly*) I'll go and get it.

(*He goes towards her bedroom, passing behind the table*)

Angele (*Quickly, passing in front of the table and taking up a position in front of the door*) No, no! There's no need to. What was the message?

Joseph I said, very respectfully, that a policeman came last night for Monsieur Champignol.

Angele (*At 2, passing behind the table and going to Joseph, who is level with it, midstage*) A policeman? What did he want?

Joseph It's about Monsieur Champignol's military service. Apparently he's been called up.

Angele My husband, one of the leading painters in Europe! Nonsense! He did his military service when he was twenty, he's never done it since. (*She comes downstage, still at 2*)

Joseph Perhaps that's why they've called him up. The policeman said he should have been with his regiment three days ago.

Angele It's too much! Do they think he's nothing better to do! Run down to the police station and say I'm very sorry but my husband's away at the moment. Explain that he's painting a portrait of Mr Vanderbilt. Remember the name. And he can't do three dozen things at the same time. He'll do his military service when he gets back.

Joseph Very good, Madame.

Angele I've never heard of such a thing. Oh, Joseph, my trunk's packed, take it downstairs. I'm going to see my nephew in Nice.

Joseph Very good, Madame.

Angele (*Pointing to the cup of chocolate on the table, right*) Take that away.

(*Joseph takes the cup and goes out into the hall. Saint Florimond appears at the bedroom door*)

t Florimond He's gone?

Angele Yes. Now, take your hat and hurry!

t Florimond (*Going towards the hall door*) Oh, with pleasure!

Joseph (*Off*) Oh, Madame!

Angele Oh! Go back in there. (*She pushes him back into the bedroom*)

(*Saint Florimond goes out. Joseph enters*)

What is it now?

Joseph It's the maid you were expecting from the country.

Angele (*At 2*) All right, later.

Joseph Oh, here she is.

(*Charlotte appears at the hall door*)

Come in, my girl, come in.

Angele (*Aside, coming downstage*) This man's driving me mad

(*Joseph goes out*)

Charlotte (*Curtsying. Strong country accent*) Madame . . .

Angele (*Sitting on the chair to the left of the right-hand table*) Ah, come here. You've been sent me by the priest at Chatellerault, an old friend of my family's.

Charlotte (*At 1, centre*) A very good man!

Angele He recommends you highly.

Charlotte So he should. I'm in an interesting condition.

Angele I beg your pardon?

Charlotte I'm in an interesting condition. My mother put me in it.

Angele Your mother?

Charlotte Yes, my mother. She sinned, my mother did. You can't know what that is in Paris. It means she was led on by a man . . . well, she sinned.

Angele Who with?

Charlotte The Fifth Dragoons. Then she went off after them and left me there, a little baby. Ill I was, too. That's when the priest said I was in an interesting condition

Angele Ah! Good! Very good! That's much better.

Charlotte He brought me up.

Angele *He* did?

Charlotte Yes . . . And my Aunt Pichu. I expect you know her son, he's in Paris. A porter.

Angele No, I've never met him. . . . Well, I don't expect you can do very much?

Charlotte Oh, yes. I can look after cows. Have you any in Paris?

Angele No. Can you sew?

Charlotte Oh, yes. I can sew, I can cook, I can dance.

Angele I'm not interested in your dancing. Have you ever served anyone before?

Charlotte Oh! I'm a virgin!

Angele (*Rising and going towards her*) That is irrelevant. Well, you seem willing, we'll try to make something of you. When my husband gets back, I hope he'll find you're a perfect servant.

Charlotte Oh! You've a man!

Angele As you say. He's away at the moment, but he should be back very soon now.

Charlotte Ah, I look forward to seeing him, bless him!

Angele Very well. I'll take you on. You'll start at forty francs a month.

Charlotte Oh, you're so kind!

Angele And board.

Charlotte Oh, you can't be bored!

Angele Now, run along.

Charlotte Yes, Madame.

(*Charlotte goes upstage. Angele crosses towards her bedroom door*)

(*Returning*) Madame!

Angele (*Turning round*) Yes.

Charlotte Would you be pleased to accept this basket?

Angele This basket?

Charlotte Yes. I thought you might like some eggs, straight from the country. I chose them myself. They're none of them fresh.

Angele Not fresh?

Charlotte No. I was told you never eat fresh eggs in Paris.

Angele Charming girl! All right, be off with you . . . What's your name?

Charlotte Charlotte. (*Aside*) I think I'm going to like it here.

(*Charlotte goes out upstage*)

Angele Phew! Now let's get rid of him. (*Going to her bedroom door and calling*) Come out.

(*Saint Florimond appears at the door*)

St Florimond It's all right now?

Angele Yes. Hurry up.

(*They both go upstage towards the door*)

St Florimond Well, I'll be off. (*Stopping upstage centre, at 2*) So this is the end of a romance that never happened. Goodbye, Angele, goodbye. (*Pause*) Angele?

Angele Yes?

St Florimond We'll never see each other again. Let me give you a farewell kiss.

Angele What!

St Florimond Not as a lover. A simple brotherly kiss.

Angele All right. As it's the last time. But hurry up.

(*He kisses her. Charlotte enters upstage*)

Charlotte Oh!

Angele, *St Florimond* Oh!

Charlotte (*Very simple*) Monsieur Champignol!

Angele, *St Florimond* What!

Charlotte (*Coming downstage to 3*) Oh, sir, I heard you'd soon be back, but I didn't know it would be as soon as this.

Angele All right, now go away. I didn't ring.

Charlotte Don't worry. I'm glad I came. (*To Saint Florimond*) Did you have a good journey, sir? You're not tired?

St Florimond Yes . . . No . . . Yes . . .

Charlotte I'm Charlotte, the new maid.

Angele (*Getting angry*) Oh! Oh! Oh!

Charlotte Now, sir, you'll be wanting to make yourself comfortable. Give me your coat.

Florimond No! No!

Charlotte Yes! Yes! With all that travelling, it must be full of dust. (*Thumping him on the back*) Look! Filthy!

Florimond Ohhh! What a way to behave!

Angele All right, stop it. Why have you come in here?

Charlotte I couldn't find my room.

Angele Well, go and wait in the kitchen.

Charlotte Oh yes, I will. (*Aside*) What a nice man! I'll go and get his dressing gown.

(*Charlotte goes out upstage*)

Angele Oh, this is too much. You heard her. She thinks you're my husband too.

Florimond It's fate.

Angele It's my fate. . . Why did you have to kiss me.

Florimond How could I know she'd come in?

Angele 'How could I know'! That's all you ever say!

Florimond Well, I couldn't.

Angele You see what happens. Come on. Do please go.

Florimond Yes, yes, I'm going. Goodbye, Angele, goodbye. For ever!

Angele Goodbye, goodbye.

(*Saint Florimond goes out upstage*)

Phew! He's gone at last. (*Coming downstage*) That girl thinks he's my husband. There's only one thing to do. Get rid of her at once.

(*Clock strikes nine*)

Nine o'clock and I'm still in a dressing gown! I've so much to do! . . . I must get dressed!

(*She passes in front of the table and goes out right. Clock finishes striking. Then a noise is heard, off. Saint Florimond bursts in*)

t Florimond The Romeos! The Romeos are here! On the stairs! Where can I hide? (*He hides behind the sofa, his head still showing above the top*)

(*Romeo enters, followed by Mauricette and Dufoulay*)

Romeo (*Italian accent*) Champignol, I say, Champignol!

All Three (*Seeing Saint Florimond*) Ah, there he is!

St Florimond (*Aside*) They've caught me. (*Aloud, going towards them*) Oh, what a lovely surprise!

Romeo (*Coming downstage to 3*) Didn't you hear us? We called you.

St Florimond (*Coming downstage to 4*) Was that you? How extraordinary! I thought it came from above. That's why I ran up . . .

Romeo (*Delighted*) It was us! Of course it was!

(*Mauricette has by now come down to 1 and Dufoulay to 2*)

Mauricette Hullo, Monsieur Champignol!

Dufoulay Hullo, Monsieur Champignol!

St Florimond (*Pretending to be pleased*) Hullo! Ah-ha! What a lovely surprise! (*Aside to audience, crossing to 4*) Well do you think it's easy to get out of a house?

Romeo (*At 3*) Ah-ha! You didn't expect us, did you?

St Florimond (*At 4*) To be absolutely frank . . . no!

Romeo There, Mauricette, I told you so!

Dufoulay (*At 2*) You see, the Army's called me up for four weeks' training.

Mauricette Delightful when you've just been married!

Romeo Be quiet, darling. It will do you both a lot of good You've no idea, Champignol, these children are disgusting, the way they carry on!

Dufoulay Well, when you've just been married, no one minds. (*He kisses Mauricette*)

St Florimond Of course not. Anyway it doesn't last long. . . . I say, wouldn't you like to come for a walk?

Romeo No, no, I wouldn't. (*He sits down, left of the right-hand table*)

Dufoulay We'd rather stay here.

(*He sits down on the sofa, left, at 2. Mauricette sits next to him, at 1*)

St Florimond (*Aside*) Ohhh! What's Angele going to say when she finds I'm still here? With the family!

Romeo You understand! We've had such a long journey and now we have to take the ten o'clock train for Clermont. That's where the poor boy has to do his service. So we said to ourselves, we've an hour in Paris, let's go and see the Champignols!

St Florimond (*At 4*) What a marvellous idea! I was just saying we never see you.

Romeo (*Rising and going downstage to 3*) Well, here we are! Here we are! (*To Dufoulay and Mauricette who are kissing each other*) Now, now, children, restrain yourselves.

Dufoulay Don't you bother about us.

Romeo By the way, what about Angèlà? (*Italian pronunciation*)

St Florimond Angèlà? (*The same*)

Romeo Of course, Angèlà. (*The same*) Your wife!

St Florimond Ah yes, Angèlà (*The same*) My wife!

Romeo Aren't we going to see her?

St Florimond Well, no, I don't think so. She's not very well.

Mauricette (*Rising and coming downstage*) Not very well?

Dufoulay (*Following her*) What's the matter?

St Florimond I don't know . . . She hasn't been well for some time . . . feeling sick . . . dizziness . . .

Romeo (*Nudging him in the ribs and laughing*) I understand. Congratulations!

St Florimond (*Aside*) What's the matter with him?

Romeo Yes, yes, I understand.

St Florimond Do you? Lucky man!

(*Angele enters, dressed*)

Angele Who is it? (*Recognising them*) Oh, no!

Romeo Ah, there she is!

Angele (*Noticing Saint Florimond*) He's here with them!

Mauricette Good morning.

Angele (*Coming downstage to 3 between Dufoulay and Romeo*) How delightful to see you! (*Aside*) This is the last straw!

St Florimond I met your uncle on the stairs. *He* brought me back.

Dufoulay Angele, good morning!

Romeo By the way! We hear you've some news for us!

Angele What is that?

Romeo Champignol told us. (*To Saint Florimond*) Didn't you?

St Florimond What? Me! Nonsense!

Romeo He's about to become a father! Congratulations, Angèlà!

Angele He told you . . .

St Florimond (*At 5*) No, I didn't.

Angele (*Furious, raising her arms to heaven*) You said that?

Romeo (*Making her lower her arms*) Don't raise your arms. Don't raise your arms.

Angele Stop it, Uncle. It's not true.

Romeo Come now! Why hide it? It's natural for a father to feel proud.

Angele No, it isn't . . . I mean, you're wrong. (*Crossing to 5, aside to Saint Florimond*) Are you out of your mind?

St Florimond Angele, I promise you . . .

(*Charlotte enters, carrying a velvet smoking jacket*)

Charlotte Here's your smoking jacket.

St Florimond (*Next to Angele, right*) Marvellous! Here's the maid!

Angele What is it now?

Charlotte (*Coming downstage to 4*) Sorry, all! I didn't know you'd got company. I've brought Monsieur Champignol's smoking jacket.

St Florimond
Angele } Oh!

Romeo Well, there's your jacket!

Charlotte Yes. Come on, sir, give me your coat.

St Florimond (*Struggling, moving to 4*) No! No!

Charlotte Yes! Yes! You must be tired after that long journey.

All Long journey?

Romeo (*At 3*) You've been away?

St Florimond Oh, not very far.

Romeo Never mind us. Put on your smoking jacket.

Mauricette (*At 1*)
Dufoulay (*At 2*) } Yes, put it on.

St Florimond (*Letting Romeo and Charlotte take off his coat*) No! No! Angele, stop them.

Angele (*Aside*) That man will drive me insane!

Charlotte (*To Saint Florimond who has put on the jacket, which is much too big for him*) There! Look, that's much better!

Romeo (*At 3*) Good heavens! You have got thin!

St Florimond (*At 4*) Thin?

Romeo (*Bunching up the jacket*) Look how big your jacket is!

St Florimond I had it made like that. It's more comfortable.

Charlotte (*At 5, taking his morning coat*) Now I'll go and brush your coat.

St Florimond No! No!

Charlotte (*Going upstage*) Yes! Yes! Of course I will! I'll put it next to Madame's bed, ready for when you get up.

(*Charlotte goes out upstage*)

Angele (*Whispering*) Look what you've done.

St Florimond (*At 4, whispering*) How could I know?

Angele (*At 5, whispering*) Don't keep on saying that.

Romeo Well, where have you been?

St Florimond Me? Nowhere. (*Recovering*) Ah, yes, yes, I've been . . . I've been painting a portrait . . . abroad . . . at Tours.

Romeo (*At 3*) A portrait? That reminds me, I've something to tell you. (*He sees Dufoulay and Mauricette, who are sitting on the sofa, kissing*) Oh really! They're kissing again. It's disgusting! Disgusting!

Mauricette Oh, father!

Romeo People don't do that in public! Look at Monsieur and Madame Champignol, they love each other, but they're not kissing all the time. They don't behave like a pair of lovers! Dammit all . . . Dufoulay, give me that sketch.

St Florimond Sketch?

Dufoulay (*Giving Romeo the sketch, stuck on cardboard, which he had brought in with him and put on the sofa*) Here it is.

Romeo (*At 3, offering it to Saint Florimond*) Here it is.

St Florimond (*At 4. Aside*) Damn, my 'Mountain Peak'! (*Laughing*) Ah! My sketch! Yes. . . Isn't it pretty?

Romeo Well, no . . . apparently it isn't. I showed it to a picture dealer. He said 'That a Champignol . . . rubbish'. I told him you'd painted it and all he said was 'Well if that's a Champignol, you'd better get him to sign it . . . that will make it worth something!' So I've brought it here.

St Florimond Sign it? (*Aside*) That would be forgery. Oh, no! (*Aloud*) No, no, I never sign sketches.

Romeo But still . . .

St Florimond No! Everyone knows that. So if I signed this one, people would say it was forged.

Romeo Would they? Then I'll put your name on the frame.

(*Romeo goes upstage and sits on the sofa, next to Mauricette and Dufoulay. They all examine the sketch*)

St Florimond Yes, do that. (*Aside*) He'll have something to boast about. (*He laughs*)

Angele There's nothing to laugh at.

St Florimond How right you are!

Angele Why won't they go? (*She passes in front of Saint Florimond and goes towards Romeo*) Uncle, you must be in a hurry, I don't want to keep you.

Romeo (*Sitting on the sofa, looking at the sketch*) What, me?

Florimond No, no, don't stand on ceremony. I'll show you out . . .

Romeo (*At 3, rising and coming downstage with the others*) Not at all, not at all! Who says I'm in a hurry? We have to catch the ten thirty train for Clermont.

(*Clock strikes the half-hour*)

Half past nine, we've plenty of time.

Angele But you must have lots of things to do . . . it's years since you were last in Paris. Have you seen the Eiffel Tower?

Romeo Yes, I've got it on my tiepin. (*Passing in front of Angele and going towards Saint Florimond*) You don't see anything else in the country. I'm fed up with the Eiffel Tower.

Florimond (*At 5*) Well, in that case . . .

Romeo (*At 4*) No, I'll stay here. I said to the children: 'We've an hour in Paris, let's go and see your cousin'. They wanted to go to a hotel . . . because, you know, they . . . but I said: 'Certainly not! People don't go to hotels in the middle of the day'.

Angele (*At 3*) How nice of you! (*Aside*) They won't go!

Romeo (*Passing in front of Angele and going to 3*) But could we possibly have a wash . . . the train, you know . . .

Angele (*At 4*) Of course. (*Aside to Saint Florimond*) This is your chance to get away. (*Aloud*) I'll show you where to go.

Romeo I wouldn't dream of it. Champignol's here, he'll take us.

Florimond (*Moving to 4*) But Angele said . . .

Romeo Angele's going to stay here. She mustn't tire herself in her condition.

(*Mauricette and Dufoulay are still upstage left*)

Angele Not again! I tell you I'm not . . .

Romeo No, you must rest. Come along, Champignol.
(*He takes Saint Florimond by the arm and goes out with him left, following Mauricette and Dufoulay*)

St Florimond Oh, dear! I am part of the family!
(*Angele has gone to the door left, and now comes back to the centre of the stage*)

Angele Oh! What a family! Someone must have had a bet! Everybody's in the plot. What a lesson! Oh, what a lesson!
(*Joseph enters*)

Joseph (*At 2*) Oh, Madame . . . I've just been to the police station.

Angele (*At 1*) All right, all right!

Joseph No, it's not all right.

Angele What do you mean? What is it? What did they say?

Joseph I told them Monsieur Champignol's not here. They said they didn't care. He'd better be.

Angele (*At 1*) What? They said . . . Oh. I'll deal with them when he gets back . . . Didn't you tell them he's painting a portrait of Mr Vanderbilt?

Joseph Yes.

Angele What did they say to that?

Joseph To hell with it!

Angele Oh!

Joseph That's what *they* said. So perhaps you'd better send Monsieur Champignol a telegram . . .

Angele (*Crossing to 2 in front of the right-hand table*) Where can I send a telegram? He's on Mr Vanderbilt's yacht. His last letter said 'At sea'. I can't address a telegram 'At sea'!

Joseph (*At 1*) But this is serious.

Angele All right! But what can they do?

Joseph I don't know. They just said 'All right, we know what to do'.

Angele Oh, you should have said so in the first place. They will!

Joseph Will they?

Angele Of course! . . . I'd never have believed it! My husband! One of the leading painters in Europe! . . . They will! All right . . . That will be all, Joseph.

Joseph I'll go and finish the shopping. There's nothing else I can do?

Angele No.

Joseph Very good, Madame.

(*Joseph goes out. Saint Florimond enters left*)

St Florimond I've got rid of them . . . I'll go now.

Angele (*At 2*) Yes. Hurry up.

St Florimond My hat!

(*He takes it and goes towards the door into the hall, still wearing his velvet jacket. Romeo enters left, with Mauricette and Dufoulay*)

Romeo Champignol, what are you doing?

St Florimond (*Aside*) They're leeches! . . . Caught again! (*Aloud*) I've something to see to. I'm going out.

Romeo Dressed like that! You are amusing!

St Florimond (*Coming down to 4, while Angele comes down to 5*) Oh! I forgot! My coat! . . . Where's my coat?

(*Bell rings*)

Oh, no! Who on earth's that?

Angele A visitor!

St Florimond Probably a model.

Romeo A naked woman!

(*Charlotte enters with Camaret, in mufti, and Adrienne*)

Charlotte Yes, Monsieur Champignol's here . . . That's him! (*She points to Saint Florimond and goes out*)

Angele Oh, no! What's she saying?

St Florimond The idiot!

Camaret (*To Charlotte*) Thank you very much.

St Florimond This is the last straw!

Camaret (*Coming down to 4, while Adrienne comes down to 5; to Saint Florimond*) Monsieur Champignol?

St Florimond (*Passing in front of Angele and reaching 6*) What! No, no! Hm! Yes, yes!

Camaret (*At 4*) Delighted to meet you. (*Pointing to Angele*) Your wife, I presume?

St Florimond (*At 6*) I presume she is!

Camaret (*Bowing to Angele*) How do you do. (*He greets the company with a circular movement of his head*) Let me introduce you to my daughter.

Adrienne (*At 5, to Saint Florimond*) I'm so glad to meet you. I adore painters. (*She shakes his hand and goes upstage towards the sofa*)

St Florimond Ohhh!

Camaret Well, now we've finished with the introductions . . . (*He sits down on one of the upright chairs by the sofa. Adrienne sits on the other*)

St Florimond (*Aside*) Now he's finished with the introductions! Who does he think he is!

Angele (*At 7, aside*) He's making himself at home! (*Aloud*) Excuse me . . .

Camaret Ah! Of course. (*Rising and introducing himself*) Captain Camaret of the 75th Infantry!

Dufoulay (*Seated on the sofa with Mauricette and Romeo, leaping up*) Stationed at Clermont?

Camaret Yes. In fact I must get back there right away. I'm in charge of the reservists.

Dufoulay Then, Captain, you're *my* captain!

Camaret Your captain?

Romeo His captain? You're his captain?

Dufoulay Yes. I'm joining your regiment.

Adrienne You're a conscript?

Dufoulay No, a reservist.

Camaret Well!

(They all sit down in the following order: Mauricette (1), Dufoulay (2), Romeo *(3), all on the sofa; Adrienne (4) and Camaret (5), both on upright chairs right of the sofa, with their backs to Angele (6) and Saint Florimond (7) who are downstage near the table)*

Florimond (*Aside*) How much longer are they going to go on gossiping? What's this captain here for?

Mauricette Captain, you must take great care of him, because he's my very own darling husband.

Camaret Indeed?

Mauricette Yes, for two whole weeks now!

Adrienne Really, you've been married for two weeks?

Mauricette Yes. (*Tapping Dufoulay on the cheek*) You're my very own darling husband, aren't you?

Romeo Really . . . Mauricette! . . . (*To Camaret*) They're disgusting . . .

Florimond (*Who has been standing apart with Angele, approaching timidly*) Excuse me, but . . .

Romeo Sh! . . . Just a moment. (*To Camaret*) You've been so kind, will you allow me to join my daughter in asking . . . you don't know who I am . . .

Camaret Monsieur?

Romeo Romeo.

Camaret Congratulations.

Romeo Be good to the boy. Keep an eye on him.

Camaret Of course. (*To Dufoulay*) Don't you worry.

Dufoulay Oh, Captain, thank you so much!

Camaret Not at all.

Mauricette There's one other thing, Captain. You must make sure he always wears a flannel vest.

Camaret (*Smiling*) Well . . .

Mauricette Oh, you must! . . . He never bothers . . . He's such a baby!

Angele (*Approaching Camaret*) This is all very interesting, but it doesn't explain why we're honoured with your visit.

Camaret Of course . . .

(He rises, followed by everyone else. Romeo and Dufoulay go upstage and look at the pictures. Adrienne approaches Mauricette, who is still at 1)

In a nutshell . . . I'm a great admirer of your husband.

Angele You're too kind.

Camaret I'm not the only one. Everybody thinks he's brilliant.

St Florimond Yes, brilliant! Brilliant!

Angele (*Aside to Saint Florimond*) Be quiet.

Camaret (*Aside*) He's not exactly modest. (*Aloud*) So there we are . . . I suddenly thought I'd ask you to do a portrait of my daughter.

St Florimond What? Me?

Camaret Yes . . . You see, I'll have to lose her some day . . . I must think about finding her a husband.

Mauricette (*At 1, to Adrienne*) You're going to get married?

Adrienne (*At 2*) Yes, I'll have to be put on the market!

Camaret (*At 3*) They've already started looking for a suitor.

Adrienne (*Aside to Mauricette*) Yes, but it's a waste of time. I've an idea of my own.

Mauricette Oh?

Adrienne Yes. Sh!

(Charlotte enters, showing in Celestin)

Charlotte He's in there somewhere.

Celestin (*Coming down to 3*) Ah, Uncle!

Camaret (*At 4, to Angele at 6*) I apologise, but this is my nephew Celestin, my sister's son.

St Florimond (*Aside; at 5*) Why does he think we're interested?

Celestin Do forgive me . . . but I was so longing to see Monsieur Champignol's studio . . .

Camaret That I ventured to invite him.

Angele I'm so glad.

Celestin (*Turning round and going upstage*) Oh, it's marvellous! Marvellous! (*He bumps into Mauricette who has gone upstage with Adrienne*) Oh! I beg your pardon.

Adrienne (*Introducing him to Mauricette*) Let me introduce my cousin Celestin.

Mauricette (*At 1*) How do you do . . .

Adrienne (*At 2. Aside*) Do you think he's handsome?

Mauricette Well . . . Not bad, certainly . . . (*Aside*) So he's what she meant by an idea of her own! (*She moves across to Dufoulay and Romeo, upstage left*)

Camaret (*Right. To Saint Florimond*) I was just saying that when my daughter gets married I'd like something to remember her by.

Adrienne (*To Celestin*) You heard! He wants to marry me off!

Celestin Yes, I heard.

Adrienne (*With a melodramatic sigh as she goes upstage with Celestin*) Never!

(*Camaret is now at 1, Saint Florimond at 2 and Angele at 3, all downstage in front of the right-hand door. The others are all upstage left, talking quietly or looking at the pictures*)

Camaret (*At 1. To Saint Florimond*) Something signed by your hand.

Florimond (*At 2*) Of course . . . I . . . (*Aside*) Ohhh! I can't paint a portrait for him!

Angele (*At 3*) Actually my husband has a lot of work at the moment.

Camaret A portrait won't take long. Anyway I don't want anything very big. (*He goes upstage and, taking the canvas which is back to front on the chair, left of the door, he returns downstage*) Something like this. (*He turns the canvas round. It's a painting of Venus emerging from the waves*)

Florimond (*Laughing*) Like that?

Camaret (*Roaring with laughter*) No, I mean that size.

St Florimond Ah, that's different.

Camaret (*Looking at the canvas*) Very funny! Is it beautiful?

St Florimond Well . . . you can see!

Camaret Oh, I've no idea . . . Pictures don't mean anything to me.

Angele But I thought you admired my husband's work so much.

Camaret I admire it because everyone else does. I mean, you don't buy pictures because you like them, you like them because you've bought them. (*He puts the canvas back on the chair*)

St Florimond Well!

Camaret (*Coming back downstage to 2*) As long as you do a good likeness . . .

Romeo (*Coming downstage*) Oh, he will. He's so clever! Would you like to see a little sketch . . .

St Florimond Oh, no! Really!

Romeo Oh, yes! Look at this.

(*He goes and gets the sketch from the sofa. Adrienne and Celestin remain upstage. The others come downstage in the following order: Mauricette (1), Dufoulay (2), Romeo (3), Camaret (4), Saint Florimond (5) and Angele (6)*)

Camaret (*Looking at the sketch*) Yes, very interesting. Especia the fat woman.

St Florimond Eh? . . . What fat woman?

Romeo (*Offended, taking the sketch and putting it back on the sofa, passing behind Dufoulay and Mauricette*) That's a mountain peak!

Camaret Ah, a mountain peak. Charming, charming! Well, Monsieur Champignol, that's all settled, so we'll come for a sitting on Friday.

St Florimond Friday . . . well . . .

Camaret You can't manage Friday? Thursday, then.

St Florimond No, no, no!

Camaret Yes, yes, yes! Delighted to have met you, Monsieur Champignol . . . and your wife . . . I'm sorry to have to rush away, but I must catch the train for Clermont.

St Florimond Of course you must.

Camaret Come along Adrienne, Celestin.

Adrienne
Celestin } Goodbye.

Dufoulay Captain, you won't forget . . .

Camaret Of course not. (*He goes upstage after Adrienne and Celestin*)

Romeo (*Following him*) We'll all see you out.

Mauricette (*The same*) Captain, you will remember to take good care of him, won't you?

Camaret Yes, yes . . .

Adrienne Goodbye, Monsieur Champignol . . . Madame Champignol . . . and . . . (*The rest gets lost offstage*)

(*They go out in the following order: Celestin and Adrienne, Camaret, Romeo, Dufoulay and Mauricette*)

St Florimond (*Right of the door into the hall*) Well! This is the . . . A portrait! I've got to paint a portrait!

Angele (*Left of the door*) What's going to happen when he comes back?

St Florimond (*Coming downstage*) I don't know . . . I'll write to him . . . I'll say I'll go to him, instead of him coming to me.

Angele (*Coming downstage*) But the portrait!

St Florimond I'll paint it. I'll take lessons.

Angele That will solve everything! . . . Oh, this is awful!

(*Romeo enters with Mauricette and Dufoulay. He comes downstage between Saint Florimond and Angele, while Dufoulay and Mauricette come down to 1 and 2*)

Romeo What a charming man! (*To Dufoulay*) You know, you are lucky to have a captain like that, he's really going to spoil you.

(*Clock strikes ten*)

Dufoulay (*At 2*) Ten o'clock already! We must say good-bye. We've only just time to catch the train for Clermont.

Romeo (*At 4*) Of course. I'm so sorry we can't stay. (*He goes to 3, passing behind Angele*) Now, Mauricette, go and get our things.

Mauricette (*Going towards the left-hand door, passing behind the sofa*) Yes, father.

Romeo (*In front of the sofa, to Saint Florimond and Angele*) I'm so sorry . . .

St Florimond So are we. (*Pushing him towards the left-hand door, passing in front of the sofa*) Do stay a little longer . . . do.

(*Romeo goes out left, following Dufoulay and Mauricette*)

Angele (*At 1*) Phew! They've gone. Now it's your turn. Go and get your coat. No, it's there, in my room.

St Florimond (*At 2*) Yes! I can't wait!

(*Saint Florimond goes out right*)

Angele (*Coming downstage right in front of the table*) Oh, what a day! What a day!

(*Charlotte enters from the hall, followed by a police sergeant and a policeman*)

Charlotte In here.

Angele The police!

Police Sgt (*Coming forward*) Where is Monsieur Champignol?

(*The policeman remains in the doorway*)

Angele Monsieur Champignol? What do you want him for?

Police Sgt (*Midstage*) My orders are to arrest Private Champignol.

Angele My husband! . . . Arrest my husband!

Police Sgt Yes. He's a deserter.

Angele (*At 2*) This is too much!

Police Sgt (*At 1*) Where is he?

Angele He's not here. He's on a boat.

Charlotte (*Who has remained upstage right, coming downstage to 3*) On a boat!

Angele Shut up, shut up.

(*Charlotte returns upstage and goes out*)

Police Sgt I'm very sorry, but in that case I'll have to search the flat.

Angele Search the flat!

(*Romeo enters left, followed by Mauricette and Dufoulay, carrying their baggage. He comes downstage to 3, in front of the sofa, while Mauricette comes down to 1 and Dufoulay to 2*)

Romeo What's all this? . . . The police?

Angele (*At 5*) It's all right, Uncle.

Police Sgt You must be Monsieur Champignol?

Romeo Me? Certainly not!

Police Sgt You're sure?

Romeo Of course I'm sure!

(*Saint Florimond enters right, fully dressed*)

Romeo (*Pointing to him*) There's Champignol!

(*Saint Florimond passes in front of the table and goes to 4*)

Police Sgt Right! (*To the policeman*) Seize that man.

All What!

Florimond Me?

Police Sgt Don't answer back. (*To policeman*) Come along, get on with it.

Angele (*At 6*) No, no, you can't! It's a mistake!

Police Sgt Very sorry, but they're my orders. I've to take Private Champignol back to his unit. He should have been there three days ago.

Dufoulay You've been called up?

Florimond No. No, I haven't.

Police Sgt What's all this? You're coming along with us!

Florimond No, no, I'm not. (*He goes left, between Dufoulay and Romeo*)

Police Sgt (*To policeman*) Go on, get hold of him.

(*The policeman comes downstage and seizes Saint Florimond*)

St Florimond Now look here . . .

Police Sgt We'll be on our way to Clermont.

All To Clermont!

(*The police drag off Saint Florimond, struggling*)

Romeo Goodbye, Angele. Oh, poor Champignol!

Dufoulay Come along, we're late.

Mauricette Goodbye, Angele.

(*They go out in the following order: Dufoulay, Maurice and Romeo*)

Angele (*Coming downstage left*) Oh, this is the last straw! Arresting *him*, instead of my husband!

(*Charlotte enters and comes downstage to 2*)

Charlotte What does it all mean?

Angele (*At 1*) It's no concern of yours. Go and get my hat and coat.

Charlotte Very good, Madame.

(*Charlotte goes out*)

Angele Yes, there's only one thing to do. I must go to Clermont. My husband's not there. Perhaps I can avoid a scandal.

(*Charlotte enters with Angele's hat and coat*)

Charlotte Here's your hat and coat.

Angele (*Putting them on*) Thank you. Now take a week's notice. And go tonight.

Charlotte (*At 2*) You're getting rid of me! . . . Why? . . . What have I done?

Angele (*Going upstage to the door*) It doesn't matter.

Charlotte (*In tears, going extreme left*) It doesn't matter! What I did doesn't matter and I'm turned into the street!

(*Joseph enters, wearing a cap. Seeing Angele dressed for the street, he stands to the right of the door, to let her pass*)

Joseph You're going out, Madame?

Angele Yes. Is my trunk downstairs?

(*Joseph nods*)

Good. I'm going to see my nephew in Nice. Don't wait up for me. (*Aside*) Oh, what a nightmare!

(*Angele goes out*)

Joseph (*At 2*) I've just heard the police have been to arrest Monsieur Champignol. Is that right?

Charlotte (*At 1, downstage left. In tears*) How should I know? I don't care.

Joseph (*Going towards her*) What's up with you?

Charlotte (*Sobbing*) What's up with me is I've been sacked.

Joseph Now, now! A lovely girl like you! (*He tries to put his arm round her waist*)

Charlotte (*Slapping his face and crossing to 2*) Take your hands off me. You're not a millionaire, are you? Well, I shan't give myself to you. I'm going to pack my bags. And collect my eggs!

(*Charlotte goes out in tears*)

Joseph (*At 1*) Poor girl! Well, I don't care. Phew! The police here for Monsieur Champignol! They must have gone away empty handed. That's going to cause a spot of bother.

Champignol (*Off*) Joseph! Joseph!

Joseph Monsieur Champignol!

(*Champignol enters, in travelling clothes, a small bag in one hand and, in the other, a paintbox, easel and camp-stool*)

Champignol Phew! Home at last! Come on, Joseph, give me a hand.

Joseph (*At 1, upstage, left of the door*) It's not worth it, sir. You must be off again at once.

Champignol (*At 2*) Off again? What on earth for?

Joseph Your military service. The police have just left. You're a deserter.

Champignol What!

Joseph (*Taking his bag, and giving him another one, which is upstage left*) Here are your things.

Champignol Where's my wife?

Joseph She's not here. Hurry up, sir, hurry.

Champignol Where's my regiment?

Joseph At Clermont, sir. The 75th.

Champignol Right, I'll be going . . . Give me a canvas, in case I have time to paint.

Joseph (*Taking one and sliding it under his arm*) Here you are, sir.

Champignol Thank you. Ohhh! I was hoping for a little peace and quiet. Oh, what a nightmare!

(*Champignol runs out*)

CURTAIN

Act II

(*Clermont: the entrance to the barracks. The next morning.*

Downstage right is a hut with a glass door. Midstage, immediately above this, is a gap, leading to the entrance to the barracks. Upstage of this is the guardroom, another hut, lying obliquely, parallel to the first, also with a door. At the back of the stage, facing the audience, is the canteen, a third hut, extending from the wings, right, to centre stage. The left-hand part of this hut forms an open shelter, containing tables and chairs.

In the right-hand part is a glass door facing the audience. An entrance between the canteen and the guardroom.
Downstage left is the front of the Hotel du Cheval Blanc, with a big entrance door in the centre, underneath a window with a balcony, to which the hotel sign is fixed. Upstage are two entrances to the stage, separated by a clump of trees. At the back of the stage, between the hotel and the canteen, is a backcloth, showing a wooded mountainous landscape with a river winding through it.
A bench in front of the canteen. Another bench on the right, between the door of the first hut and the entrance to the barracks.
When the curtain rises, the Reservists *are standing in two ranks facing the audience. They are wearing a wide variety of clothes. The front row from left to right consists of a* Reservist, Lafauchette, Lavalanche, *the* Prince of Valence *and* Badin, *with five* Reservists *in the rear rank.*
Lieutenant Ledoux *stands downstage with a list of names in his hand, taking the roll call.* Sergeant Belouette *stands immediately upstage of him*)

Ledoux Dubois!
Reservist Sir!
Ledoux Planchet!
Reservist Sir!
Ledoux Champignol! (*Pause*) Well? Champignol!
Belouette (*At 2*) Under arrest, sir!
Ledoux Ah, yes. The deserter brought in by the police yesterday. Benoit!
Reservist Sir!
Ledoux Pincon!
Reservist Sir!
Ledoux Lafauchette!

Lafauchette (*Very urbane, elegantly dressed, with a bowler hat. Taking a step forward and saluting*) Here I am.

Ledoux Here I am! What do you mean, here I am?

Lafauchette I mean I'm here.

Ledoux Don't be impertinent, you in the bowler hat! Didn't you hear everyone else say 'sir'?

Lafauchette I thought . . .

Ledoux You don't think, you say 'sir'!

(*Lafauchette falls back into the ranks*)

Dufoulay! (*Pause*) Dufoulay! Well, where is he?

Belouette Dufoulay! Dufoulay!

(*Mauricette runs out of the hotel, followed by Dufoulay, in civilian clothes, and Romeo*)

Mauricette Oh heavens, the roll call! Hurry up, you'll be punished. (*She pushes Dufoulay past her*)

Dufoulay (*Going to 3*) Coming! Coming!

Ledoux Oh, you've arrived, have you?

Romeo (*Going to 3*) Let me apologise for him. I'm his father-in-law.

Ledoux (*Passing behind Romeo and going to 3*) Get to hell out of here.

Romeo Very good, sir.

Mauricette (*Embracing Dufoulay*) Goodbye, darling.

Dufoulay Goodbye, angel.

Ledoux Hey, you over there! Haven't you finished yet?

(*Dufoulay falls in, between the Reservist and Lafauchett[e] in the front rank*)

Romeo (*To Ledoux, pointing to Mauricette and Dufoulay*) They're lovebirds . . . lovebirds.

Ledoux What did you say?

Romeo (*Taken aback*) Nothing. (*Passing in front of Ledoux, Dufoulay and Mauricette, and going towards the hotel*) Come, Mauricette. That officer's not very polite.

(*Romeo goes out into the hotel, followed by Mauricette. As she goes out, she blows a kiss to Dufoulay. Ledoux is facing her and thinks it's addressed to him. Flattered, he salutes her, then turns round and finds himself face to face with Dufoulay, who is also blowing a kiss, which he receives)*

Ledoux Try to restrain yourself a little! (*Pause*) You'd better start by being more punctual.

Dufoulay I was with my wife, sir.

Ledoux (*Still at 1, extreme left. Belouette is at the extreme right*) When you're a soldier, you haven't a wife. They're for civilians. Come along. Fall in! Lucky for you the Captain's not here!

Dufoulay The Captain won't say anything to me. We're great friends.

Ledoux Silence!

Dufoulay I was with him all yesterday.

Ledoux Silence, I said! How do I get men like this? (*Crossing to Belouette*) Three days ago we had the Territorials. Now we've the Reservists. Will it never end?

Dufoulay (*Aside to Lafauchette, who is next to him*) I'll get the Captain to deal with him.

Lafauchette A good job too!

Camaret (*Off*) Adjutant! . . . Where's the Adjutant?

Ledoux The Captain!

(*Camaret enters midstage right from the barracks and goes to 2*)

Camaret (*To Ledoux*) Ah, there you are! I've just been round the barracks. The rooms aren't swept, the beds aren't made, the mess tins are filthy.

Ledoux (*To the Reservists*) Do you hear, you lot!

Camaret I don't want any 'you lot'. I'm talking to you, Adjutant!

Lafauchette (*Aside*) Good, it's his turn now.

Camaret (*To Lafauchette*) Stop laughing, you there, number 4. (*To Ledoux*) Don't let me have to tell you again, right?

Lafauchette (*Aside to Dufoulay*) The captain sounds a bit difficul

Dufoulay No, a splendid fellow. I'll put in a word for you.

Lafauchette Thanks very much.

Camaret (*To Ledoux*) Ah! These are the reservists?

Ledoux Yes, sir.

Dufoulay (*Who has been signalling to the Captain. Aside*) Very odd! He doesn't seem to recognise me. (*He waves again and coughs to attract attention*)

Camaret You there, Tom Thumb, what's the matter with you?

Dufoulay I was just saying hullo, sir.

Camaret Ah, you were just saying hullo. (*To Ledoux*) Give that man two days C.B. for saying hullo to an officer.

Dufoulay (*Aside*) He doesn't recognise me. (*To Camaret*) Dufoulay!

Camaret Exactly. Dufoulay. Adjutant! This man's kind enough to give you his name: Dufoulay. Make it four days.

Dufoulay That's a bit tough.

Lafauchette (*Aside to Dufoulay*) Don't you put in a word for me

Camaret (*To Ledoux*) What are you doing?

Ledoux Taking the roll call, sir.

Camaret Right. Carry on.

Ledoux Benoit!

Reservist Sir!

Ledoux Pincon!

Reservist Sir!

Ledoux Lafauchette!

Lafauchette Sir! (*He takes a step forward and salutes*)

Camaret Get back in the ranks. (*Going to Lafauchette*) He looks a cut above the others. Your job?

Lafauchette Stockbroker.

Camaret (*Scornfully*) A parasite! Pah!

(*He goes downstage left, near Ledoux, who is still at 2*)

Lafauchette (*Aside*) Parasite!
Camaret (*To Ledoux*) Go on, get on with it.
Ledoux Dufoulay!
Dufoulay Sir!
Ledoux Bloquet!
Reservist Sir!
Ledoux Valence!
The Prince (*Taking off his hat*) Excuse me, Prince.
Camaret Prince! What do you mean 'Prince'?
The Prince Prince of Valence.
Camaret You're a prince, are you? What do you do apart from that?
The Prince Nothing.
Camaret Ah, you're a prince and you do nothing. (*To Ledoux*) Well, we'll have to find something for this prince to do. (*He comes downstage centre*)
Ledoux Badin!
Badin (*A fat man in an overcoat and top hat*) Sir!
Camaret (*Turning round and going towards him*) Good God! You look splendid, you do!
Badin I'm fine, thank you, Captain. How are you?
Camaret I'll show you how I am – in the guardroom! Your job?
Badin I sell tickets.
Camaret What sort of tickets?
Badin Er – all sorts of tickets.
Camaret Ah, if it's impossible to get seats anywhere, you make money, touting outside on the pavement. Adjutant! Any trouble from him and we'll stick him inside for a change.
Ledoux Very good, sir. Lavalanche!
Lavalanche Sir!
Camaret (*To Lavalanche, who is holding a bag*) Well, young man, don't let me see you clutching your baggage again. This is a parade ground, not a railway station.

Right, we'll cut the rest of the roll call. Form a circle!

(*Reservists form a semicircle. Ledoux is at the extreme left, Belouette extreme right. Camaret is in the centre*)

We are destined to spend four weeks together. A lot of you, I'm sure, arrive with preconceived ideas; scared stiff. I'm here to tell you you're wrong. You must remember the regiment's just one big family. Your officers in effect are official fathers. The colonel's the father of his regiment, the captain, father of his company. In other words I shall be your father.

Lafauchette (*Aside*) Nice fellow!

Camaret (*In the same tone*) If you make a mistake at drill, you'll get two days C.B. If you answer back, three days. If you've a dirty uniform, you'll get two days in the guardroom. If you're drunk, a week. And so on.

(*Everyone is thunderstruck*)

Now I rely on you not to cause me any trouble and you can rely on me to make your tour of duty as pleasant as possible.

Lafauchette (*Aside*) Splendid!

Camaret (*In the same tone*) Adjutant! Give that man two days in the guardroom, for not listening.

Ledoux Very good, sir.

Camaret Right. Carry on.

Ledoux In two ranks, fall in!

(*The Reservists do so, upstage as before*)

Camaret (*To Ledoux*) See if the quartermaster's ready to issue uniforms.

Ledoux Very good, sir.

(*Ledoux goes out upstage right, between canteen and guardroom, passing behind Camaret*)

Camaret Stand easy!

(*He signals to Belouette to join him and they talk quietly during the following lines*)

Dufoulay Phew!

Lafauchette Difficult chap, this captain of yours.

Dufoulay Yes. But he's quite different socially.

Badin (*Looking to the right*) Who's this NCO coming along now?

The Prince He's a major.

(*Belouette salutes Camaret and goes upstage right, in front of the Reservists. Fourrageot enters midstage right, from the barracks*)

Fourrageot Where's Captain Camaret?

Camaret Here, sir.

Fourrageot (*Going to Camaret at 2*) Well, Captain, you've got all your reservists?

Camaret Yes, sir.

Fourrageot They haven't drawn their uniforms yet?

Camaret I've just sent down to the quartermaster, sir.

Fourrageot (*Passing in front of Camaret and going to 1*) Good, good, good.

(*Ledoux enters upstage right, between guardroom and canteen and comes downstage*)

Camaret (*To Ledoux*) Well?

Ledoux All ready for them, sir.

Camaret Very good. Take them along.

Fourrageot (*To Camaret*) Right, I'll inspect them in an hour's time.

Camaret Very good, sir.

(*Fourrageot goes out midstage left, behind the hotel*)

Ledoux Squad, shun! By the left, quick march!

(*Reservists go out upstage right, between guardroom and canteen, Ledoux and Belouette marching alongside*)

Camaret Left, right, left, right! Get into step, number five! My God, DuFOOLay! Get into step, will you!

(He follows them to the extreme right. Angele enters from the hotel)

Angele Oh, I haven't slept a wink all night . . . All this excitement . . . I must see Saint Florimond . . . I couldn't send him a note, with those dreadful policemen . . . (*Noticing Camaret who is coming downstage*) Oh, Captain!

Camaret Madame Champignol! When I saw you in Paris yesterday, I never expected I'd have the pleasure of seeing you again today.

Angele Captain! I want to ask you a great favour.

Camaret I can guess. You're going to ask if you can see your husband.

Angele My husband! Exactly.

Camaret Actually, he's under arrest. How did he manage to forget about being called up?

Angele Oh, you know, Captain, artists are so absent-minded.

Camaret Of course . . . Of course . . . I must say, what you're asking is strictly illegal. Well, for you, I'll break the rules for once.

Angele Oh, thank you, Captain.

Camaret (*Looking to the right*) Here come the men under arrest. On fatigues. I'll get him for you. (*Going upstage right and calling*) Corporal Grosbon!

Grosbon (*Off*) Sir!

(Grosbon enters upstage right, between guardroom and canteen)

Grosbon Yes, sir?

Camaret This lady would like to speak to her husband, Private Champignol . . . He's under arrest . . . Send him here.

Grosbon Very good, sir.

(Grosbon goes out right)

Angele Oh, Captain, how kind of you!

Camaret (*Passing in front of Angele and going towards the hotel*) I do apologise, but duty calls . . .

Angele Of course.

Camaret (*After saluting, as he goes into the hotel*) Get me a vermouth.

(*Grosbon enters upstage right, between guardroom and canteen*)

Grosbon Come along, get on with it. Quicker than that! Why do I have to get saddled with a fool like this!

(*Saint Florimond enters, wearing dirty ragged fatigues and a torn cap. He is painfully pulling a wheelbarrow*)

Florimond All right, Corporal, all right. Angele!

Angele You!

Florimond (*To Grosbon*) You might have told me not to bring my barrow.

Grosbon This lady's asked for you, so I'll leave you here. I'll come and collect you in a few minutes.

Florimond Yes, yes. (*He sets down his barrow centre stage*)

(*Grosbon goes out upstage right, between guardroom and canteen*)

Angele You! Dressed like this!

Florimond (*Coming downstage to 2*) Yes. (*Aside*) Oh, it's embarrassing to be seen like this by the woman you love. (*Aloud*) Yes . . . these . . . these are fatigues. You know, the last twenty-four hours haven't been exactly funny!

Angele Do you think it's been funny for me? Anyway, up to now, luckily, everything's all right.

Florimond All right! Do you think I've been enjoying myself? Dragged off by policemen like a pickpocket! Right across Paris on foot, surrounded by jeering urchins! I met friends from the Club, who said 'Oh' and looked the other way. Do you think that's nice? I couldn't explain to them. A crowd collected. One wretched little man began telling everyone I'd been murdering children. I thought they were going to throw me in the river.

Angele How dreadful!

St Florimond Do you think it's any better here? I was vaccinate Vaccinated! You know I can't stand a pinprick. It itched all night! Then they made me sleep on bare boards with a lot of men who'd been very badly brought up. I've been bitten all over.

(*He rubs his sleeve. Angele recoils*)

It's all right, they've gone now. Then this morning the most revolting fatigues. Now I've a wheelbarro but that's nothing. You don't know what Army latrines are like. I hope you never will. Oh, no! I've had enough. Enough! (*He goes upstage and sits down in the barrow*)

Angele (*Going towards him*) Cheer up. Four weeks will go in a flash.

St Florimond (*Rising, appalled*) Four weeks? You expect me to stay here for four weeks?

Angele You made people think you were my husband. Yo must keep it up to the end.

St Florimond No, I can't. I've other engagements. (*He comes downstage to 2*)

Angele (*Following him at 1*) Nonsense! They're not important.

St Florimond This evening there's Madame Rivolet's ball! I'm due to meet this girl with lots of money!

Angele I won't stop you going to the Ball. It's here in Clermont, so if you can get leave . . . All I ask, no I insist, is that you do my husband's military service through to the end.

St Florimond Ohhh! I'll never get caught again!

Angele Nor will I. (*Laughter off*) Sh! Someone's coming.

(*They go into the hotel doorway and talk there. Lavalanche, Lafauchette, The Prince, Badin and the other Reservists enter upstage right, between guardroom and canteen. They are all in uniform except Badin who is still in civilian clothes, complete with top hat*)

Lavalanche (*The first to enter, pointing to Lafauchette who follows*) Take a look at this maternity dress! (*Pointing to the Prince who is next*) And the Prince is even worse!

The Prince (*Coming downstage right*) These uniforms are disgusting. Disgusting!

Lafauchette (*Noticing Angele who is still talking to Saint Florimond*) Look! A pretty woman! Prince!

The Prince Yes.

Lafauchette Do you know her?

The Prince Who? No, never seen her before. That surprises me. (*To Badin*) Do you know who that lady is?

Badin No. (*To Reservist*) Do you?

Reservist No.

(*Dufoulay enters upstage right, between guardroom and canteen, wearing a uniform that is much too big for him. He comes downstage, passing through the group of Reservists*)

Dufoulay Oh, what a uniform!

Lafauchette Hey, there! Perhaps you can tell us. Who's that pretty woman over there?

Dufoulay Where?

All (*Pointing to Angele*) There! There!

Dufoulay Talking to Champignol? Why, it's his wife!

All His wife!

Dufoulay She happens to be my cousin by marriage.

The Prince Introduce me.

All Introduce all of us.

Dufoulay (*Going towards Angele*) Good morning, Angele.

Angele, *St Florimond* (*Aside*) Dufoulay!

Dufoulay (*To Saint Florimond*) Good morning. (*Introducing*) Angele . . . my comrades! Gentlemen, my cousin

Madame Champignol and her husband!

Reservists (*In a group, right, saluting*) Good morning.

St Florimond (*Aside*) Ohhh! That man's a fool! A fool!

(*Bugle call off. Belouette enters right and comes downstage centre*)

Belouette Come on there, get back into barracks.

(*The Reservists go out into the first hut, saluting Angele*)

(*To Dufoulay*) Including you, Tom Thumb!

Dufoulay (*Bumping into the barrow*) Coming, Sergeant, coming. (*To Saint Florimond and Angele*) See you later.

(*He goes out into the first hut, followed by Belouette*)

Angele (*To Saint Florimond in front of the hotel*) Then that's settled. I'll go back to Paris tonight, to be there when my husband comes home. I won't tell him he's been called up, you'll take his place and everything will be all right.

St Florimond You twist me round your little finger.

Angele Monsieur de Saint Florimond, you're a very gallant gentleman.

(*She goes out into the hotel*)

St Florimond (*Coming downstage*) A very gallant gentleman! Gallant, yes, but fed up! Oh, I'll never forget my affaire with Madame Champignol. (*He falls, sitting, into the barrow*)

(*Grosbon enters upstage right, between guardroom and canteen*)

Grosbon Hey! What are you up to? You were allowed to talk to your wife. Now it's over, get on your way!

St Florimond Very good, Corporal. (*Going upstage, pulling the barrow*) Oh, what a life! What a life!

(*Champignol enters quickly midstage left, behind the hotel. He is carrying a suitcase in one hand and, in the other, his painting equipment; a canvas, paint-box, easel and campstool*)

Champignol Ah! Here at last! I must be posted as a deserter!

(He bumps into Saint Florimond, who is going upstage, pushing his barrow)

Florimond Look where you're going, can't you!

Champignol I am sorry.

Grosbon Come along there!

Florimond Yes, Corporal.

(Saint Florimond goes out upstage right between guard-room and canteen, passing behind Grosbon)

Champignol (*Calling*) Excuse me, Corporal.

Grosbon (*At 2*) What do *you* want?

Champignol (*At 1, saluting*) Champignol, Corporal, Champignol!

Grosbon Champignol? Under arrest.

(Grosbon goes out right, between guardroom and canteen)

Champignol (*Coming downstage*) Under arrest! I should have expected it. The whole thing's unbelievable. Maybe the first three days was partly my fault; I was away. I know that's none of their business. But I might have been here yesterday, if it hadn't been for the call-up papers. They tell me to report to Clermont. I've never heard of this Clermont, all I know is Clermont-Ferrand. So I went there. They might have given more details. I've been searching for the 75th Infantry all over Clermont-Ferrand. Ohhh! If I told them, they wouldn't believe me. They'd laugh. Now I'm overdue and under arrest. Under arrest! I'm finished!

(Ledoux enters from the first hut, right)

Ledoux What are you doing there?

Champignol (*At 1. Aside*) An officer! (*Aloud*) I'm Champignol, sir.

Ledoux Ah, you're Champignol! The deserter. Well, why aren't you in the Guardroom? You're under arrest.

Champignol Under arrest! I'm finished. (*Louder*) Finished!

Ledoux I didn't know it was finished. In that case, get

back into barracks. (*He passes behind Champignol goes upstage left*)

Champignol What? . . . Very good, sir. (*Aside*) What did that Corporal mean? It doesn't matter. (*Going out*) I thought there'd be more trouble than this.

(*Champignol goes out into the first hut*)

Ledoux (*Left*) He's pretty dense. Probably just a country bumpkin.

(*Camaret enters and stands in the hotel doorway*)

Camaret Adjutant!

Ledoux Sir.

Camaret Are your men properly dressed now?

Ledoux Yes, sir.

Camaret Get them on parade. I'll inspect them.

Ledoux Very good, sir.

(*Ledoux goes out upstage right, between guardroom and canteen. Camaret goes back into the hotel. A bell rings offstage. Belouette, Grosbon, and all the Reservis enter hurriedly from the first hut. They are in uniform except for Badin who is as before*)

Belouette Squad! Fall in! Get on with it!

(*The Reservists fall in, facing the audience in two rank The front row, from left to right, consists of Corporal Grosbon, Dufoulay, Lafauchette, Lavalanche, Badin, the Prince. When they have fallen in, Camaret enters from the hotel*)

Camaret (*To Badin*) What the devil are you doing in civvies

Badin They couldn't find clothes to fit me, sir.

Camaret Clothes! You don't wear clothes!

Badin Well, an outfit.

Camaret You don't wear outfits! What do you call it when everyone's dressed alike? When they're dressed uniformly, what do you call it?

Badin Er . . . Livery.

Camaret Livery! (*To Belouette, who is at 2, right*) Give that man two days in the guardroom. If you're dressed uniformly, you're wearing a uniform! Bloody fool!

Badin I can see I'm going to enjoy myself!

Belouette Company, shun!

(*Champignol enters from the first hut*)

Champignol (*Aside*) Ohhh! On parade already! (*To Belouette*) Where do I go, Sergeant, where do I go?

Belouette Your usual place, of course!

Champignol My usual place! Oh, God!

(*He rushes into the squad, treading on the Prince's toes. The Prince yells. Then he tries to take Lavalanche's place*)

Lavalanche No, not here!

Champignol Oh, I see. (*He tries to take Dufoulay's place*)

Dufoulay You're not here!

Belouette Have you quite finished dancing around there?

Champignol (*Squeezing sideways into the ranks between Dufoulay and Lafauchette*) All right, all right. You can carry on now, Sergeant.

Belouette Squad, number!

(*The Squad starts to number: 1, 2, 3, 4*)

Champignol 4B.

Belouette Squad, open ranks, march!

Camaret (*Moving forward*) Everyone's on parade?

Belouette Yes, sir.

Camaret Let's have a look at them. (*He inspects them, starting from the left. To the first man*) Your neckband goes round twice, not once. (*He lifts up the next man's jacket, and sees he is not wearing braces. The same with Dufoulay*) You're not wearing braces. Weren't you told to wear them?

Dufoulay Yes, sir, but they hurt me.

Camaret Oh, they hurt you. (*To Belouette, who is at 1*) Change those four days C.B. to two days in the guardroom for making subversive remarks.

Dufoulay But I thought . . .

Camaret You're not here to think. And shut up.

Dufoulay (*Aside*) He doesn't seem to like me.

Champignol This captain seems a bit strict.

Camaret Right! Now, Corporal, you can start drilling your squad.

Camaret (*To Belouette*) By the way, Sergeant, get me Private Champignol.

Champignol Me! (*He steps forward out of the ranks*) Sir!

Camaret (*At 3*) What's the matter with you?

Champignol But I . . .

Camaret You're not a Sergeant, are you? Well, get back in the ranks.

Champignol Oh! Very good, sir. (*Taking his place in the squad*) The man's mad!

Camaret Hurry up, Sergeant.

(*Belouette goes out upstage right, between guardroom and canteen*)

Camaret (*Aside*) I've had an idea. I've got Champignol here so I'll make him paint my portrait. (*Aloud*) Carry on, Corporal, I'm going to see if the barrack rooms look any better.

(*Camaret goes out into the first hut*)

Grosbon (*Back to the audience*) Squad, shun! Form two ranks.

(*They do so, finishing with, from left to right in the front rank, Champignol, Dufoulay, Lafauchette, Badin, Lavalanche, the Prince. The rear rank consists of six Reservists*)

Right dress!

(*They do so, carefully leaving a little space between each, to allow freedom of movement*)

Grosbon Eyes front! Now remember you're not here to enjoy yourselves. Any nonsense and I'll have you in the guardroom. Squad, shun! Horizontal movement of the arms, keeping the elbows straig

In two motions, like this. One, two! One, two!

Reservists (*Executing the movement*) One, two! One, two!

Grosbon All together. That's feeble . . .Feeble! (*To Champignol*) You there, you're feeble!

Champignol (*Aside*) If Mr Vanderbilt could see me now!

Grosbon Squad, halt! (*Running to Champignol*) Can't you hear me?

Champignol Sorry, Corporal. I didn't understand.

Grosbon Didn't understand? Is there something funny about the way I talk?

Champignol (*Aside*) It's too awful to be funny.

Grosbon You there, in civvies! You can't do this in a top hat!

Badin Very good, Corporal. (*He takes off his hat and, not knowing where to put it, keeps it in his right hand and carries on with the exercise*)

Grosbon Squad, shun! Horizontal and lateral movement of the arms, with elbows straight and knees bending. Like this. One, two! Begin!

Champignol (*As he does it*) This is ridiculous. God, this is ridiculous!

Reservists One, two! One, two!

(*Romeo enters from the hotel, followed by Mauricette. He has a fishing rod on his shoulder and a fisherman's basket hung round his body*)

Romeo Do come along, Mauricette.

Mauricette (*Coming downstage to 1*) Oh, Father . . . look at them.

Dufoulay (*Noticing her*) My wife!

Mauricette (*Signalling to Dufoulay*) Do look, Father. He's doing it much better than anyone else.

Dufoulay (*Aside*) God, how embarrassing doing this in front of one's wife!

Grosbon Squad, halt! (*Seeing Mauricette*) Oh, a pretty face! (*To the Reservists*) Come along, try to do it properly. You've got a gallery.

(Badin puts his hat down on the ground)

Mauricette Oh, Father, I want to kiss him.

Romeo I shouldn't. This is not the moment.

Grosbon Squad, left turn!

(They do so, except Dufoulay who turns right)

Right turn!

(They turn back, facing the audience. Dufoulay turns the other way, finishing with his back to the audience)

Just look at that idiot there.

Mauricette
Romeo } Oh!

(Dufoulay turns round, facing the audience)

Grosbon Don't you know your left from your right, you bloody fool?

Dufoulay He calls me a bloody fool in front of my wife!

Mauricette Oh! I won't have anyone talking to my husband like that!

Romeo Keep out of this. Don't read the Riot Act to the Army.

Dufoulay Let me tell you, Corporal . . .

Grosbon 'Let me tell you, Corporal'! Just look at him. I advise you not to get married, no wife's going to stay faithful to you.

Dufoulay Oh!

Mauricette
Romeo } Oh!

Grosbon *(To Romeo, who is next to him)* Just look at him. I've never seen such a fool.

Romeo *(Stepping forward)* He's my son-in-law.

Grosbon Oh! He's your . . . Hm . . . Squad, right turn! . . . Quick march! . . . Double march!

(Badin picks up his hat and puts it on, then they all double out midstage left, behind the hotel)

Mauricette *(At 1)* Oh, Father! Did you hear how that awful man spoke to my husband?

Romeo Don't worry. It doesn't mean a thing in the Army. They always talk like that. Well, you don't feel like coming fishing with me?

Mauricette No. We've an introduction to a Madame Rivolet, I'll go and call on her. We have to stay here four weeks, we might as well get to know people.

Romeo All right. Run along.

Mauricette Goodbye, Father. (*She goes out left, behind the hotel*)

Romeo The river's next to the hotel, I'll go and try a cast or two. I saw one or two pools this morning where I think I might catch something.

(*Camaret enters from the first hut*)

Camaret The barrack rooms are filthy. Where's the Sergeant?

Romeo (*At 1*) Oh! The captain!

Camaret (*Going downstage to 2*) Signor Romeo! Where are you going in that get-up?

Romeo I'm going fishing. Perhaps I shall have an enormous tench.

Camaret I'm sure you won't smell at all.

Romeo Not enormous stench! Enormous tench!

Camaret Oh, an enormous tench.

Romeo That's what I said, enormous tench.

Camaret Yes, yes, I see. By the way, you haven't seen your nephew, Champignol?

Romeo No.

Camaret (*Going upstage right*) Well, what's he doing? I sent for him.

(*Saint Florimond enters midstage right, from the entrance to the barracks. He is now in ordinary uniform. Belouette enters with him*)

Florimond What does the Captain want me for?

Belouette I don't know. He'll tell you. (*He points to Camaret*)

Camaret Ah, there you are. Good.

Romeo (*To Saint Florimond*) Hullo, prisoner!

Florimond (*Aside. Moving to 2*) Prisoner! (*Aloud*) Hullo, hullo!

Camaret (*At 3, to Belouette who is at 4*) Sergeant! I've just been round the barrack rooms. They're almost the same as they were an hour ago. Filthy dirty and personal belongings all over the beds. You know I won't have that. Do something about it.

Belouette Very good, sir.

(*He goes out into the first hut. Romeo has been talking to Saint Florimond*)

Camaret Champignol! Come here.

St Florimond Sir . . .

Camaret As you're not just anyone, I'm going to do you a great favour.

St Florimond Me, sir?

Camaret I'm excusing you all fatigues.

St Florimond Oh, sir!

Camaret Instead you're going to get your brushes and paint my portrait.

St Florimond What!

Camaret I said you're going to paint my portrait.

St Florimond I thought you did. (*Aside*) That's the last straw!

Camaret What are you waiting for?

St Florimond I'm very honoured, sir, of course, but I can't. I can't.

Camaret Why can't you?

St Florimond Well . . .

Camaret You refuse?

St Florimond No, sir, no. I haven't any brushes. Or anything else. It's all in Paris.

Camaret Damn! How infuriating!

St Florimond Yes, sir, I'm terribly disappointed. Of course, if I had my things here . . . I'd be delighted . . . I'd start right away.

Camaret Damn, damn, damn!

Romeo Yes . . . it's a sad business (*pronounced peessiness*) . . . a sad peessiness.

(They slowly cross to extreme left in a line, still in the same order. Belouette enters from the first hut)

Belouette Everything's put away in the barrack rooms now, sir. This was all I could find. It seems to be a painter's things . . . a canvas, a paintbox, . . . *(He is also holding an easel and a campstool)*

All What!

Camaret A paintbox!

Belouette *(At 4)* Yes, sir. It belongs to Champignol. His name's on it.

Camaret *(To Saint Florimond)* What an earth were you saying just now? *(To Belouette)* All right, leave it all here. Good. Now go and get someone to sweep out the rooms.

Belouette They're all on parade, sir.

Camaret Well, go and get one of them off parade.

(Belouette passes behind Camaret and goes out midstage left, behind the hotel)

What the devil were you talking about? You hadn't any . . .

t Florimond But, sir, I didn't know. I've no idea where all this came from. I didn't bring it. Perhaps my wife wanted to give me a surprise. Anyway, it's here, that's a fact, it is here.

Camaret Yes, that's the main thing. Now you can start work on my portrait.

Romeo *(To Saint Florimond)* Yes, isn't that lucky! You were so disappointed . . .

(Romeo passes in front of Saint Florimond and picks up the painting equipment, which he carries back to the left, passing again in front of Saint Florimond)

't Florimond Oh, do shut up.

Camaret *(At 3)* Right. Now get everything ready. *(He goes back upstage)*

't Florimond *(At 2, undoing the bag)* Ohhh! What a situation!

Romeo (*At 1, putting up the easel and setting out the stool*) I'll give you a hand.

St Florimond No, no. There's no hurry.

Camaret (*Coming downstage to 3*) What do you mean, 'No hurry'? Come along, how are you going to do me?

St Florimond (*Aside*) That's what I was wondering.

Camaret How shall I pose? Is this all right? (*He assumes a pose*)

St Florimond Hm . . . er . . . I think I'd prefer it if you were sitting.

Camaret Good idea! I'd prefer it too, from the posing point of view . . . Go and get me a chair.

St Florimond Right away, sir.

(*Saint Florimond goes out into the hotel. Camaret and Romeo wait on the steps. Belouette enters midstage left, behind the hotel, with Champignol*)

Belouette Come along.

Champignol All right, Sergeant. What's all this about?

(*Belouette goes out into the first hut*)

Ah, an easel! . . . It's mine! These are my things! They're very free and easy here. (*He picks everything up, puts it under his arm and goes towards the first hut, right*)

Camaret (*Still on the steps*) Hey! What's the matter with you? Are you mad?

Champignol (*Turning back*) Well, sir . . .

Camaret Ah, it's our comedian. Trying to get yourself noticed. Put those things down.

Champignol But, sir . . .

Camaret I told you to put them down.

(*Champignol, grumbling, puts them back where they were*)

Now get to hell out of here.

Champignol This is tyranny. Tyranny!

Camaret How do we get hold of buffoons like this?

(*Belouette enters from the first hut*)

Belouette Hey, you!

Champignol Yes, sergeant.

Belouette (*Genial*) You haven't eaten anything yet today, have you?

Champignol No, Sergeant, no, I haven't.

Belouette (*Taking a broom from inside the hut, and giving it to him*) Well, get a bellyful of this. Sweep out the hut.

Champignol Me?

Belouette Yes. Get a move on.

Champignol Ohhh! If Mr Vanderbilt could see me now!

(*He passes in front of Belouette and goes out into the hut. Belouette follows him. Camaret and Romeo have been opening the paintbox, preparing brushes, etc. Saint Florimond enters from the hotel with a chair*)

St Florimond Here's the chair.

Camaret Ah! Thank you.

St Florimond (*Aside*) Oh, God! God! Inspire me.

(*Camaret sits down at 1, midstage, level with the hotel door. Saint Florimond sits on his stool at 2, with the easel in three quarters view, so that the canvas is visible to the audience. This canvas must be white and the actor must draw as best he can. Romeo stands behind him, still holding his fishing rod*)

Camaret (*Already seated, assuming a pose*) Like this? Full face?

St Florimond Hm! No . . . In profile . . . (*Aside*) Now I've only half his face.

Camaret I'd prefer it full face.

St Florimond I'm not asking what you'd prefer. I prefer the profile.

Camaret (*Showing his right profile*) This one?

St Florimond No, the left . . . That's better. (*Aside*) Left out altogether would be better still.

Camaret Right . . . Are you ready? . . . (*Giving an order*) Begin!

St Florimond (*Settling down at the easel*) Ohhh! What am I going to do? (*Starting to sketch*) Sometimes desperation works miracles.

Romeo (*Behind him*) Very good! . . . What's that?

St Florimond His nose.

Romeo I thought it was the peak of his cap.

St Florimond Think what you like . . . but don't bother me. (*He goes on drawing. Aside*) Ohhh! He'll never believe it's a Champignol!

(*Champignol enters from the first hut, sweeping away*)

Champignol They're turning me into a charwoman! Oh, another painter! (*Coming down to 4*) Hm! He's not up to much

Romeo (*At 3, still behind Saint Florimond*) I say! What's that?

St Florimond (*Impatiently*) His eye. Damn!

Romeo Oh! His eye! (*To Champignol*) It's very interesting, watching someone painting. Not bad, eh?

Champignol (*Making a face*) Yes. He looks like a primitive.

Romeo Possibly, possibly.

Champignol (*Shyly, approaching Saint Florimond, passing in front of Romeo*) I say . . . A bit too widely spaced . . . his eye and his ear.

St Florimond What did you say?

Champignol A bit too widely spaced . . . His eye and his ear.

Camaret (*Posing*) What is it now? (*Turning his head*) You again! Tell the sergeant to mark you down for two days C.B.

Champignol (*Aside*) Me! (*Passing in front of Romeo and going towards the first hut, right*) Whenever I say anything . . . Marvellous! . . . He always picks on me . . .

Camaret Didn't you hear?

Champignol Yes, sir. (*Going into the hut*) I won't open my mouth again.

(*Champignol goes out into the first hut*)

Romeo It's funny . . . to judge by his sketches you'd never think he could paint a pretty picture.

Camaret Phew! . . . I'm getting a stiff neck . . . Are you nearly finished?

't Florimond As you wish, sir.

Camaret (*Rising, passing behind the easel and coming downstage to 2*) All right, that's enough for today. Let's have a look.

't Florimond Ohhh! What's he going to say?

Camaret (*Looking at the canvas on the easel*) That's me?

't Florimond Yes . . . Yes . . . It's . . .

Camaret (*Picking up the canvas and examining it*) Phew! If I look anything like that . . .

't Florimond It's . . . It's . . . the first sketch. You know, simply a guide for the painter. It doesn't mean anything to anyone else.

Camaret Is that so? I must say it doesn't mean anything to me.

't Florimond You won't see this eventually.

Camaret Right. You can put your things away.

(*Saint Florimond does so during the next few lines*)

Romeo I think it's going to be very good.

Camaret I hope so, because at the moment . . .

Romeo Now . . . I'm going fishing . . . (*To Camaret*) You're not coming?

Camaret No . . . Thank you.

Romeo Then I'll see you later.

(*Romeo goes out upstage left. Camaret goes out with him for a moment. Saint Florimond puts his things away, picks them up in one hand and, with the other, collects the chair and goes out into the hotel. Reservists enter midstage right from the barracks*)

Reservists Ah, a break at last. (*Etc.*)

(*Reservists go towards the first hut*)

Grosbon Hey, steady there! Not so fast! Who's coming with me to get the potatoes?

Reservist (*At 3*) I will, Corporal, if you like.

Grosbon (*At 2*) What's your job?

Reservist Unloading vegetable carts.

Grosbon Then stay here. (*To the Prince*) What about you?

The Prince (*At 1*) I'm the Prince of Valence.

Grosbon A prince? . . . Go and get the potatoes.

(*The Prince goes out midstage left, behind the hotel. The others remain in a group upstage. Saint Florimond enters from the hotel, carrying his things. Camaret enters upstage left*)

St Florimond I'll be going now, sir. (*He crosses to the right*)

Camaret Right. By the way, your hair's too long. Get it cut.

St Florimond (*Aside*) What a life! (*Aloud*) Very good, sir.

(*Saint Florimond goes out midstage right, into the barracks. Ledoux enters from the first hut*)

Camaret Adjutant! Private Champignol's hair's too long. Get it cut.

Ledoux Very good, sir.

Camaret Right away!

(*Camaret goes out into the hotel*)

Ledoux Where is Champignol?

(*Champignol enters from the first hut*)

Ah, there he is! (*To Belouette*) Sergeant! Get that man's hair cut.

Champignol (*At 2*) Me?

Belouette (*At 3*) Very good, sir.

(*Ledoux goes upstage left*)

Champignol But, Sergeant, my doctor won't allow it.

Belouette I didn't ask for your opinion.

(*Grosbon enters from the first hut*)

Corporal! Get that man's hair cut.

(*Belouette goes out downstage right*)

Grosbon Very good, Sergeant. (*Calling*) Barber!

Champignol But, Corporal . . .

Grosbon Shut up.

(*The Barber enters from the first hut*)

Barber Corporal?

Grosbon Cut that man's hair.

(*Grosbon goes upstage left*)

Barber Very good, Corporal. (*To Champignol*) Come along then.

Champignol This is awful. Awful!

(*Champignol goes out into the first hut, followed by the Barber. The Prince enters midstage left with an enormous sack of potatoes on his back*)

Grosbon Come along, you prince there, get moving.

The Prince (*Crossing the stage*) Ohhh! I feel as though the whole of Society's staring at me.

Grosbon Put it down there.

(*The Prince does so, downstage right*)

Now everyone, get into those potatoes.

(*The Reservists gather round the sack and start peeling the potatoes*)

Ledoux (*Left*) I'm going to smoke a cigarette. (*He goes upstage left*) Oh, a fisherman! He'll never catch anything. I'll go and have a look. (*Ledoux goes out upstage left*)

(*Chatter from Reservists, gradually dominated by:*)

Lavalanche (*Singing to the tune of Alouette*)

Oh, potatoes,
We all peel potatoes.
Peel potatoes
Every bloody day.
I will pluck out all the eyes

All We will pluck out all the eyes. (*Etc.*)

(*A shout, off. Ledoux re-enters and comes downstage*)

Ledoux Help! Help! Quickly! Help!

Reservists What is it?

Ledoux That fisherman's fallen in the river! Hurry! Hurry!

Dufoulay I bet it's my father-in-law.

Lavalanche A man in the river! Good! That's finished potato peeling.

Reservists Hurry! Hurry!

(*Reservists rush out*)

The Prince (*Downstage. Not moving*) Hurry! Hurry!

(*Camaret enters from the hotel*)

Camaret What's happened? What's all this shouting?

The Prince (*Still downstage. Very calmly*) A fisherman's fallen in the river.

Camaret What! And you stand there! Run and help! Where is this fisherman? Where is he?

(*Romeo enters upstage left, supported by Dufoulay and surrounded by Ledoux and the Reservists. He is soaked to the skin and sneezing, as though he has swallowed a lot of water*)

Ledoux Come along. This way. This way.

Dufoulay Come along, Father.

Camaret (*At 1*) Signor Romeo!

Romeo (*At 2. Sneezing*) Atchoo! Atchoo! I'm drowned! I'm drowned!

Camaret It's really you, Signor Romeo?

Romeo Captain! Oh, Captain! What a plunge! Let me tell you all about it.

Camaret No, you can do that later. You can't stay like this. You're soaked. (*To Reservists*) Take him into barrac and rub him down. (*To Romeo*) Would you like a drink?

Romeo Yes. Something hot and strong.

Ledoux I'll go and get it for you.

(*Ledoux goes out into the canteen*)

Dufoulay Come along, Father.

Romeo (*Going out midstage right, into the barracks*) Oh, what a plunge! What a plunge!

(*Romeo goes out, sneezing*)

Camaret Phew! A fine state he's in!

(*Saint Florimond enters upstage right, between guardroo and canteen*)

Ah, there you are! Just in time! Your uncle's fallen in the river.

Florimond (*Coming downstage to 2*) My uncle? I haven't an uncle.

Camaret What! You haven't an uncle! . . . Signor Romeo!

Florimond Oh, Romeo! . . . He's . . . He's my wife's uncle. That's why I . . . Oh, he's fallen in the river. Well, well, well! (*Pause. Unconcerned*) Is he dead?

Camaret What! Is he dead? A fine nephew you are! No, he's not dead, just soaked to the skin. So hurry up, will you!

Florimond Yes, yes, yes.

Camaret Good god, your hair! Is that how they've cut it?

Florimond (*Taking off his cap*) No, they haven't yet.

Camaret What! Not yet!

Florimond Oh, poor uncle! Fallen in the river! Well, well, well! (*Saint Florimond goes out into the first hut*)

Camaret They haven't cut his hair yet! This is too much. I'll deal with that adjutant.

(*Ledoux enters from the canteen and comes down to 2*)

Ledoux Here's the drink.

Camaret Adjutant! I thought I told you to get Private Champignol's hair cut.

Ledoux Yes, sir . . . It's being done now.

Camaret Bloody lies! Take two days C.B. for not obeying my orders.

Ledoux But, sir . . .

Camaret Be quiet! . . . That's enough!

(*Camaret goes out into the hotel*)

Ledoux Damn you, Champignol! Right! Just you wait!

(*Champignol enters from the first hut and comes downstage to 2. His hair is slightly shorter*)

Champignol Phew! They've just cut my hair!

Ledoux So there you are! I told you to get your hair cut!

Champignol (*Taking off his cap*) It's just been done, sir.

Ledoux Bloody lies! To start with, you've just got me

confined to barracks. Take two days C.B. (*Crossin[g] to midstage and calling*) Sergeant!

(*Belouette enters from the first hut*)

Belouette (*At 3*) Sir!

Ledoux I thought I told you to get this man's hair cut!

Belouette It's just been done, sir.

Ledoux Bloody lies! Take three days C.B. for not obeying my orders.

(*Ledoux passes behind Champignol and goes out downstage left*)

Belouette Ah, you get me confined to barracks, do you? Ta[ke] three days C.B. Just a moment. Corporal Grosbo[n]

(*Grosbon enters from the first hut and comes downstag[e] to 3*)

Grosbon Sergeant!

Belouette I thought I told you to get that man's hair cut!

Grosbon It's just been done, Sergeant.

Belouette Bloody lies! Take four days C.B. for not obeying my orders.

(*Belouette goes out upstage right*)

Grosbon (*Passing to 2*) Ah, you get me confined to barracks do you? Take four days C.B.

Champignol (*Aside*) That makes nine.

Grosbon Just a moment. Barber!

(*The Barber enters from the first hut*)

Barber Corporal! (*He comes downstage to 3*)

Grosbon I thought I told you to get that man's hair cut!

Barber I've just done it, Corporal.

Grosbon Bloody lies! Take four days C.B. for not obeying my orders.

Barber Oh! (*Aside*) That's a bit steep.

Grosbon Go and crop that man's head. Now!

(*Grosbon goes out*)

Barber (*At 2*) Well! That's pretty mean of you. Getting a pal into trouble!

Champignol A pity he can't give me any C.B. I was beginning to get used to it.

Barber Come along then.

(*The Barber goes out into the first hut, followed by Champignol. Dufoulay enters midstage right, from the barracks, with* Romeo, *Lafauchette and the Prince*)

Dufoulay Well, Father, are you all right now?

Romeo (*In uniform. Coming downstage to 2*) Ah, that's better. It's very good of you all to lend me these clothes.

All Not at all.

Dufoulay I've taken yours to the cookhouse to dry out.

Romeo These don't seem to fit very well.

Dufoulay You look like a very new recruit!

Romeo It was a silly business (*peessiness*) falling in the river like that.

Dufoulay How did it happen?

Romeo (*Sitting down on the bench. Everyone gathers round him*) Well, I was on the river bank. But you can't cast very far from there. Then I saw a tree trunk sticking out of the water. I jumped onto it and splash! I fell in!

(*Everyone laughs. Grosbon enters midstage right, from the barracks, running*)

Grosbon The C.O. . . . The C.O.! Hurry up, you lot! Get back into barracks!

All The C.O.! Oh!

(*Reservists rush out into the first hut, jostling* Romeo. *Grosbon follows them. An uproar can be heard inside*)

Romeo (*Midstage*) What was all that? Well, I don't care. It's nice here. The sun's coming out. Just right after a swim. (*He lies down on the bench in front of the canteen*)

(*Fourrageot enters from the barracks, a cigar in his mouth, and comes downstage right*)

Fourrageot Nobody here! Damn this cigar, it keeps on going out. Extraordinary! The Colonel gave it me. (*He takes a box of matches out of his pocket and lights his cigar*)

Romeo (*Singing*) 'O sole mio . . .'

Fourrageot (*Turning round*) What the devil's that?

Romeo (*Singing*) La, la, la, la, la.

(*Fourrageot sees Romeo and goes slowly up to him. Romeo goes on singing. Fourrageot stands firmly in front of him*)

Fourrageot A reservist! What are you doing there?

Romeo (*At 1*) Hullo, hullo!

Fourrageot (*At 2*) Hullo! He says hullo to me! What the devi are you doing? Who do you think you're talking to? Who do you think you're talking to?

Romeo Hullo, hullo!

Fourrageot Are you deaf, man? Are you saying hullo to me?

Romeo Hullo! Yes.

Fourrageot You lout, you! Will you stop this nonsense!

Romeo Who is this extraordinary man?

Fourrageot Stand up! Have you ever seen a man lying down i front of his commanding officer? Come on, stand up!

(*Romeo shrugs his shoulders, lies down again and goes on singing. Fourrageot, furious, takes him by the collar and drags him downstage right to 2*)

Will you stand up!

Romeo Really! Do leave me alone.

Fourrageot What did you say? Do you realise I'm going to put you in prison?

Romeo Don't talk rubbish.

Fourrageot You're not back in your farmyard now, you peasant. Trying to be clever, eh? You don't know me. I'll tame you.

Romeo Now, now, now! I'll tell you what happened. (*As talks, he takes a bit of fluff off Fourrageot's uniform*)

Fourrageot Stand to attention! (*He slaps his hand*)

Romeo (*Crossing to 1*) Oh, really! This man's so rough! There's no talking to you. You will keep on yelling all the time.

Fourrageot Sergeant! Who the devil's this man?

(*Belouette enters midstage right, from the barracks and comes downstage to 3*)

Belouette I don't know, sir. He must be a reservist arrived this morning.

Fourrageot Ah, that's it! Nothing military about him! You've never been a soldier of France, have you?

Romeo No, I'm Italian.

Fourrageot Ice-cream wallah! I'm not surprised. What's your name?

Romeo Romeo.

Fourrageot Sergeant, put Romeo down for four days C.B.

Romeo Me?

Fourrageot Detail a corporal to take this man and read the Manual of Discipline to him for the next hour.

Belouette Very good, sir.

Fourrageot (*Going towards the first hut*) You don't know me, you lout. I'll tame you.

(*Fourrageot, still muttering, goes out into the hut*)

Grosbon (*Off*) Squad, shun!

Romeo (*At 1*) That sergeant seems rather rude.

Belouette (*At 2*) Silence!

(*Ledoux enters midstage right, from the barracks*)

Wait here while I speak to the Adjutant.

(*He goes behind Romeo towards Ledoux*)

Ledoux (*Coming downstage to 1, a letter in his hand*) Just my luck! My little milliner's free tonight and thanks to Champignol, damn him, I'm confined to barracks.

Belouette (*Coming downstage to 2*) Sir! One of the men on guard is ill. I need a replacement.

Ledoux (*Passing to 2*) A replacement! Take Champignol.

Belouette (*Passing behind Ledoux and going towards Romeo*) Champignol. Very good, sir.

Ledoux I'll make him pay for this.

Belouette (*To Romeo*) Come along, you.

Romeo Where?

Belouette You'll see.

(*They go out midstage right, into the barracks*)

Ledoux (*Coming downstage*) After all, at night the adjutant's in command. I'll do my C.B. at my milliner's hous

(*Champignol enters from the first hut and comes downstage to 2. His hair is cropped close*)

Champignol Phew! I've certainly been cropped all right.

Ledoux Ah, there you are. Have you had your hair cut?

Champignol Oh, yes, sir. (*Taking off his cap*) Is that all right now?

Ledoux That will do. Now go and get changed. You're on guard.

Champignol Me?

Ledoux (*Passing behind him and going towards the hut*) Yes, you! Hurry up.

(*Ledoux goes out*)

Champignol It never rains but it pours!

(*He follows Ledoux into the hut. Romeo enters midsta right, from the barracks, followed by Grosbon*)

Romeo For heaven's sake! What's it all got to do with me Leave me in peace.

Grosbon (*Reading*) 'If any other rank . . .

Romeo (*Coming downstage to 2*) Ohhh!

Grosbon (*At 1. Continuing*) . . . 'wishes to speak to an officer when carrying a rifle, he will salute in accordance with the Small Arms Manual.'

Romeo (*In desperation shrugging his shoulders, raising his eyes to heaven and starting to hum*) La, la, la, la.

Grosbon You don't seem to be listening to what I'm saying.

Romeo Yes, yes.

Grosbon You're carrying a rifle, an officer passes . . . what do you do?

Romeo Hm. Well . . . I fire.

Grosbon You fire! Is that how you listen?

Romeo What? No. How do I know? (*Passing to 1*) You stand there jabbering away. I'm not interested. Leave me in peace.

(*Mauricette enters midstage left, behind the hotel*)

Mauricette Father! Where are you?

Romeo Mauricette!

Mauricette (*Coming downstage to 1*) Father! You're in uniform!

Romeo You see, I fell in the river.

Mauricette You fell in the river!

Romeo Yes, but everything's all right now.

Grosbon (*Ignoring the conversation and going on reading*) 'If an other rank speaks to an officer and is not carrying a rifle . . .'

Romeo I was standing on the bank . . .

Grosbon '. . . he springs smartly to attention . . .'

Romeo I saw a tree stump sticking out of the water . . .

Grosbon '. . . and salutes in the usual manner.'

Romeo Oh, for heavens sake! For heavens sake! I can't hear myself speak!

Grosbon I was told to read you the Regulations.

(*Dufoulay enters from the first hut, carrying Romeo's clothes. He comes downstage to 4*)

Dufoulay Here are your clothes, Father. They're dry now.

Romeo My clothes! There! You can see I'm not a soldier!

Grosbon These are the Sergeant's orders.

Dufoulay Well, the Adjutant's orders are that he's to change into civvies.

Grosbon Oh, if it's the Adjutant . . .

(*Grosbon goes out upstage right, between guardroom and canteen*)

Romeo Have you been to Madame Rivolet?

Mauricette I left our cards and the letter.

Romeo Good, good. Come along then, children.

(*They go out into the hotel. Immediately before they go out, Belouette enters midstage right, from the barrac followed by Saint Florimond in dress uniform, the chinstrap of his cap underneath his chin*)

St Florimond I have to go on guard?

Belouette You're Champignol, aren't you? The Adjutant said 'Put Champignol on guard'.

St Florimond What a damned nuisance! Sergeant!

Belouette Well? What is it?

St Florimond Do I have to stay here?

Belouette Of course you have to stay here.

St Florimond No, I mean where is my beat?

Belouette From there to there. (*He points to the whole depth of the stage from the first hut to the canteen*) And from there to there. (*He points to the area from the canteen to the wings, right*)

St Florimond Very good, Sergeant.

(*Belouette goes out into the guardroom. Saint Florimon mounts guard, first across the width of the stage, then disappearing between guardroom and canteen. Ledoux enters from the first hut, followed by Champignol, dressed for guard duty*)

Ledoux Are you ready, Champignol? Right. You can go on sentry duty straight away.

Champignol Where, sir?

Ledoux Here of course.

(*Ledoux goes out midstage left*)

Champignol Very odd! . . . I've only just arrived . . . And on guard already! (*He marches up and down from the first hut to the canteen. As he goes back the second time, he comes face to face with Saint Florimond who is coming back downstage*) Another sentry!

St Florimond Another sentry!

Champignol What are you doing?

’t Florimond They’ve put me on guard.

Champignol Me too.

’t Florimond Oh . . . How funny!

Champignol Very funny!

(*They march up and down the stage from front to back in opposite directions*)

’t Florimond You’re a Reservist?

Champignol Yes? And you?

’t Florimond Me too.

Champignol How do you do?

’t Florimond How do you do?

(*They shake hands, then resume their beat*)

Champignol I say . . . Weren’t you painting the Captain’s portrait just now?

’t Florimond Yes. I was.

Champignol You’re an artist then?

’t Florimond No, I’m not. I’ve never held a brush in my life. That’s what’s so awful.

Champignol How is that?

’t Florimond It’s like a novel.

Champignol A novel? (*Taking his arm*) I like a good story.

(*They continue their beat, arm in arm, their rifles at the slope*)

’t Florimond Well . . you see . . . It’s very serious . . . An intrigue with a married woman . . . and professional discretion . . .

Champignol Go on, go on. I won’t tell anyone.

’t Florimond I won’t mention the lady’s name . . . Well . . . you see . . . (*Going upstage arm in arm as before*) For several weeks I’ve been pursuing a married woman.

Champignol Pretty?

’t Florimond Enchanting! . . . But there’s absolutely nothing between us.

Champignol That’s what people always say.

St Florimond No, I promise you.

Champignol (*As they come downstage*) Oh, come on! All right, we'll say nothing happened.

St Florimond Oh, it did.

Champignol There! You see!

(*They both halt arm in arm, facing the audience, Saint Florimond still at 1, Champignol at 2*)

St Florimond No, you don't understand. What happened was I was mistaken for the husband. I'm here in the Army instead of him.

Champignol No! How terribly funny! Some husbands have all the luck! It's never happened to me! But tell me, why were you painting the Captain's portrait, if you've never held a brush before?

St Florimond Oh, I haven't told you. The lady's husband . . .

Champignol Well?

St Florimond He's a painter.

Champignol Another painter? How amusing!

St Florimond Another painter?

Champignol Of course! You don't know me. I'm Champignol.

St Florimond (*Jumping in the air and going into bayonet drill*) In! Out! On guard! (*Falling terrified on the bench in front of the canteen*) It's him! Him! (*Turning it into a cough*) Ahim! Ahim!

Champignol Bad cough you have, old man! (*Slapping him on the back, then sitting next to him*) Well . . . what about you?

St Florimond Me? . . . What?

Champignol What's your name?

St Florimond Er . . . Augustus.

Champignol Augustus . . . what?

St Florimond Augustus . . . nothing. Illegitimate!

Champignol My dear fellow, I am sorry. But don't let that worry you. Look at the Roman Emperor . . . he was just Augustus, like you. But that didn't affect his career.

Florimond No, it didn't.

Champignol (*Rising*) Augustus! Go on . . . tell me. This painter . . . well? . . . In confidence . . . what's his name?

Florimond (*Rising*) Oh, no! No! I can't!

Champignol (*Taking his arm*) Come on. I'm longing to know.

(*They continue their beat, arm in arm as before*)

Florimond Oh, you say that . . . !

Champignol I'm not just being inquisitive, I may know him.

(*They halt downstage*)

Florimond Well . . . it's . . . Raphael.

Champignol (*Laughing*) Nonsense! He's been dead for over three hundred years.

Florimond Wait. You won't let me finish. Raphael Potard!

Champignol Raphael Potard! Extraordinary! A painter . . . called Potard. Never heard of him.

Florimond Oh, he's not well known. Not at all well known. (*Going upstage with Champignol*) He married a mulatto . . . a mulatto . . . She had negro blood.

Champignol (*Coming downstage*) Naturally.

Florimond Well, this mulatto . . .

(*Fourrageot enters from the first hut, as they come downstage arm in arm*)

Fourrageot What! What the blazes is this? What do you two think you're doing?

Champignol (*At 1*)
Florimond (*At 2*) } (*Halting*) Sir?

Fourrageot Where have you ever seen anyone mount guard like that? And present arms when you see me!

(*Fourrageot passes to the left* (*1*). *Champignol and Saint Florimond turn face to face and present arms*)

Not like that!

(*Champignol does a half turn. They then find themselves one behind the other and present arms like that*)

Where do they find these men? Why are there two of you?

St Florimond I don't know, sir . . . They detailed us . . .
Champignol Yes, Augustus and me . . .
Fourrageot Augustus! . . . Sergeant!
(*Belouette enters from the guardroom and comes downstage to 4*)
Who are these men? Why are there two of them?
Belouette (*Dumbfounded*) I don't know, sir. I only detailed this one. (*He points to Saint Florimond*)
Fourrageot (*To Champignol*) Well, what do you think you're doing?
(*Belouette goes upstage in front of the canteen*)
Champignol I don't know, sir. I was detailed by the Adjutant.
Fourrageot The Adjutant! . . . Get back into barracks!
Champignol (*Aside*) Delighted!
Fourrageot And don't let me catch you at it again.
Champignol (*Aside*) He seems to think I did it for pleasure. (*Aloud*) Goodbye, Augustus.
(*Champignol goes out into the first hut*)
Fourrageot (*To Saint Florimond*) As for you, try to behave a bit better when you're on guard. What's your name?
St Florimond (*At 2*) Me? I don't know any more.
Belouette (*Coming downstage between them*) He's Private Champignol, sir.
Fourrageot Champignol. (*To Belouette*) Keep an eye on this man when he's on guard. Right, dismiss!
(*Belouette salutes and goes out into the guardroom*)
(*To Saint Florimond*) Take your cap off.
(*Saint Florimond does so*)
Your hair's too long.
St Florimond I've been told so already, sir.
Fourrageot Well, get it cut then!
St Florimond (*Going upstage and resuming his beat*) Very good, sir. Ohhh! Her husband here! Her husband!
(*Saint Florimond goes out upstage right, between*

guardroom and canteen, still on sentry duty. Ledoux enters midstage right, from the barracks)

Fourrageot Adjutant!

Ledoux (*Coming downstage to 1*) Sir!

Fourrageot (*At 2*) Get Champignol's hair cut.

Ledoux (*Dumbfounded*) Shorter?

Fourrageot Naturally. Not longer! Don't make silly remarks. (*He passes to 1*)

Ledoux (*At 2*) Yes, sir.

Fourrageot You understand, eh?

(*Fourrageot goes out midstage right, into the barracks*)

Ledoux Why is everybody making such a fuss about Champignol's hair? Well, why should I bother?

(*Champignol enters from the first hut with the barber. He has got rid of his pack and rifle*)

Champignol Come along. I'll give you a drink for all the trouble I've caused you.

Ledoux (*At 1*) Ah, Champignol! Come here.

Champignol (*At 2*) Sir! (*Aside*) What is it now?

Ledoux Let's see your hair.

(*Champignol takes his cap off*)

Right! Barber! Go and cut Champignol's hair.

Champignol Again!

Barber (*At 3*) But, sir, I've put the clippers all over his head!

Ledoux Well shave it then. I'm not going to have any more trouble. Go on, take him away.

(*Ledoux goes out midstage right, into the barracks*)

Champignol (*Upset*) Oh . . .

Barber Come on, you.

Champignol I'm being disfigured! Disfigured! I won't have a hair left.

(*He goes out into the first hut with the barber. Saint Florimond, still on duty, enters upstage right, between guardroom and canteen and comes downstage right*)

St Florimond Her husband! That's the final blessing!

(*Ledoux enters. Saint Florimond ignores him*)

Ledoux (*At 1*) Sentry! What do you do when you see me?

St Florimond (*At 2, presenting arms*) Is this right?

Ledoux No, that's presenting arms. But it will do.

(*Ledoux passes in front of Saint Florimond and goes out into the first hut*)

St Florimond What's going to happen? Oh, I know. A scandal. An appalling scandal! There's only one thing to do. Champignol's here. So let them sort it out. I've this ball tonight. As soon as my guard's finished, I'll vanish.

(*Celestin enters left*)

Celestin I say, Sentry, where's Captain Camaret?

St Florimond (*Midstage at 2*) I haven't seen him, sir.

Celestin (*Coming downstage to 1*) If I'm not mistaken . . . Monsieur Champignol!

St Florimond The Captain's nephew!

Celestin What a surprise!

(*They shake hands. Camaret enters from the hotel*)

Camaret What! Go on, Sentry, make yourself at home.

Celestin Uncle!

Camaret (*Coming downstage to 1*) Oh, it's you!

Celestin Yes. I was just asking Monsieur Champignol . . .

Camaret Champignol on guard! You're under arrest! What are you doing on guard?

St Florimond I don't know, sir.

Camaret Sergeant!

(*Belouette enters from the guardroom*)

Belouette Sir! (*He comes down to 4*)

Camaret Sergeant! What's the meaning of this? Men don't go on guard, if they're under arrest! I let him off fatigues, that's all. Relieve him at once and lock him up.

Belouette Very good, sir. (*To Saint Florimond*) Come along, you *'t Florimond* (*Going upstage*) Lock me up! (*Aside*) How shall I get to the ball? (*To Belouette*) All right, I'm coming. I know the way.

(*Saint Florimond goes out into the guardroom with Belouette*)

Celestin (*At 1*) Poor Monsieur Champignol!

Camaret (*At 2*) Pah! Well, what's brought you here?

Celestin Mother wants you to come early this evening. With Adrienne.

Camaret Why is that?

Celestin The ball. Adrienne will have to be the hostess. Mother's ill.

Camaret Very well. What's the matter with her?

Celestin Oh, nothing serious. A bout of gout.

Camaret What?

Celestin Her gout. She's had another bout of it.

Camaret She's rather stout for gout. But there's a lot of it about.

Celestin No doubt.

(*Camaret goes upstage with Celestin. Champignol enters*)

Champignol How dare they mutilate anyone like this!

(*He takes off his cap, wraps his head in his handkerchief, and puts his cap back on top*)

Camaret (*Upstage left*) What! What the devil's that man doing with a bald head? Hey, you there!

Champignol (*Reaching midstage*) Sir?

Camaret (*Coming downstage to 2, while Celestin comes down to 1*) Show me your head.

Champignol (*Taking off his cap*) Look. Would you believe it?

Camaret Would I believe it! Oh, it's our funny man.

Champignol (*Proudly*) He's recognised me.

Camaret How dare you have your hair cut like that! Do you think you've the right to turn your head into a marble?

Champignol But sir . . .

Camaret Take two days in the guardroom. That will teach you not to make yourself grotesque.

Champignol Oh, no! This caps everything.

Camaret Dismiss. Get back into barracks. And stay there till your hair's grown again.

Champignol Yes, sir. (*Aside*) I've had enough of this. Oh, they'll drive me mad. First they shave my head, then they throw me in prison.

(*Champignol goes out into the first hut*)

Camaret That's typical. Leave them alone for one moment and all they think about is making themselves ridiculous. (*He passes in front of Celestin and goes to 1*)

(*Angele enters from the hotel*)

Angele (*Speaking into the wings*) Yes, do, please.

Celestin Madame Champignol!

Angele (*Coming downstage to 1*) Excuse me, Captain, but could you tell me where I can find out the times of the trains?

Celestin (*Saluting*) Good afternoon.

Angele Oh, forgive me, I didn't recognise you.

Camaret They must have a timetable in the hotel. You really mean to leave us?

Angele Yes. I'm going back to Paris this evening.

Celestin Why don't you stay one more day? My mother, and all of us, would be delighted if you'd come to our ball tonight.

Angele Your mother?

Camaret Yes, Madame Rivolet. My sister.

Angele (*Aside*) His sister!

Camaret She's giving a small dance . . . for my daughter Adrienne. They're going to introduce her to a suitor – a Monsieur de Saint Florimond.

Angele (*Aside*) Saint Florimond! And the Captain's daughter! Oh! Poor man!

Celestin Can't you really come?

Angele Oh no, impossible! Absolutely impossible!

Celestin I am sorry.

Camaret So am I. I hope you have a good journey.

(*He salutes and goes upstage left with Celestin*)

Angele (*Aside*) I've got to see Saint Florimond. If he goes to this ball, everything's ruined. (*Aloud*) Captain . . .

Camaret Yes?

Angele I must ask you for yet another favour. Before I go, I'd like to say goodbye to my husband.

Camaret (*Upstage*) Of course.

(*Ledoux enters upstage right, between guardroom and canteen*)

Adjutant!

Ledoux Sir!

Camaret Go and get Champignol and tell him his wife's asking for him.

Ledoux (*Going out*) Very good, sir.

(*Ledoux goes out right*)

Camaret (*Saluting*) Now I must be going . . .

Celestin (*Bowing*) Good afternoon . . .

Angele Goodbye. Goodbye, Captain; thank you.

(*Camaret goes out midstage left, behind the hotel, with Celestin*)

Oh, thank heavens I was warned in time!

(*Dinnertime is sounded on the bugle. The Reservists enter, running, from the first hut and disappear upstage right, between the guardroom and canteen*)

Reservists Dinner's ready. About time too. (*Etc.*)

(*Ledoux enters midstage right, from the barracks and is jostled by the Reservists*)

Ledoux Look where you're going! (*To Angele*) Here's Private Champignol.

Angele Thank you so much.

Ledoux (*To Champignol, off*) Come along then.

(*Champignol enters midstage right, from the barracks. Ledoux goes out*)

Champignol A lady's asking for me?

Angele (*At 1*) My husband!

Champignol (*Coming downstage to 2*) My wife! You're here! Angele, darling! How good of you to come!

Angele Yes. I thought . . . They said . . . (*Aside*) Oh, I feel faint.

Champignol I was going to write . . . Why are you staring at me like that? . . . Oh, my hair? (*Taking off his cap*) Could you believe they'd do this to me? I'm bald, darling, I'm bald!

Angele (*With a forced laugh*) How funny! (*Aside*) He's going to learn the truth.

(*During this scene the Reservists have returned one by one with their mess tins. Some sit down on the benches upstage, others go back into the hut*)

Champignol Angele, darling . . . Let me kiss you.

Lavalanche (*On one of the canteen benches*) Just look at that. A soldier's kissing Madame Champignol.

Reservists (*Crowded upstage*) Oh!

Badin Phew! What about her husband?

(*Saint Florimond enters midstage right, from the barracks*)

St Florimond Done it! There was a flimsy wooden door and I broke it down. I've escaped.

Reservists Here he is.

Angele (*Aside*) Saint Florimond!

Lavalanche (*Going to Saint Florimond*) Hey! Who's that fellow talking to your wife?

St Florimond I don't know him.

Lavalanche You don't know him! . . . He's kissing your wife!

St Florimond Ah, he . . . Well, well, well! He . . . he must be . . a relation of hers.

Lavalanche (*To the Reservists*) He's a relation of hers!

Reservists (*Sarcastically*) Oh!

'hampignol (*To Angele*) Where are you staying? The hotel?

Angele Yes. There!

'hampignol Good. (*To the Reservists*) I say, we don't have to sleep in barracks, do we?

Reservists No, no.

'hampignol Splendid. Because of course I'd rather spend the night with Madame Champignol.

All Oh!

Florimond (*Falling onto the right-hand bench*) Ohhh!

Angele Ohhh!

'hampignol Come along, darling . . . Take me to your room.

(*Reservists laugh*)

Angele This way. (*Aside*) What a nightmare!

(*Angele and Champignol go out into the hotel*)

Florimond (*Rising and going midstage, followed by the Reservists*) Well, who am I meant to be? Who am I meant to be?

avalanche Well? . . . Did you hear? . . . She's taking him up to her room!

Florimond (*At 2*) Yes. Yes.

avalanche (*At 3*) You don't say anything?

Florimond Oh! Oh! That man has certain rights. The fact is, he's . . .

avalanche The fact is he's your wife's lover, dammit. That's obvious.

Florimond My wife's lover!

avalanche You've got it, old man, you've got it.

(*The Reservists go upstage, laughing*)

Florimond I've got it! I've got it! (*Aside*) Champignol's getting on my nerves. He's making me look a fool. I seem to be the deceived husband. No, that's silly, because it's as Champignol . . . so he's the one . . . He's deceiving himself! Ah well, I don't care. I'll get into my own clothes and when I'm seen again, it won't matter.

(*Saint Florimond goes out into the first hut*)

Lavalanche (*Upstage*) Look, he's going. Watch out.

Badin He's amazing.

All (*Laughing*) Marvellous! (*Etc.*)

(*Lafauchette, the Prince and other Reservists enter midstage right, from the barracks, carrying their mess tins*)

Lavalanche Come here. You don't know what we've just seen

Reservists No. What?

Lavalanche Champignol. You know, Champignol . . . he's und arrest. Well! His wife's sleeping with another man!

Reservists No!

Lavalanche Yes! One of us!

(*Laughter*)

Come on, Badin, Pincon, let's go and tell everybod

(*They go out midstage right, into the barracks*)

Reservists (*Laughing*) Marvellous!

(*Champignol enters from the hotel*)

Champignol (*Coming downstage to 1*) What's the joke?

Lafauchette (*At 2*) We've just heard a wonderful story. You know Champignol?

Champignol Champignol?

Lafauchette His wife's sleeping with another man!

Champignol What!

The Prince (*At 3, roaring with laughter*) One of us reservists!

Champignol (*Furious*) Where is this man? Where is he?

(*Saint Florimond, in civilian clothes, enters from the first hut*)

St Florimond Ah, I'm ready now.

The Prince Look. There he is!

Champignol What! Augustus! . . . Ha! So I was Potard! (*Falling on him*) And you're my wife's lover!

St Florimond (*At 2*) Let go of me.

Champignol (*At 1*) You'll pay for this!

Reservists What does he mean?

(Romeo appears on the hotel balcony with Mauricette and Dufoulay)

Romeo A battle!

All Separate them.

(Angele enters from the hotel and comes downstage)

Angele Heavens! My husband and Saint Florimond!

(They separate Saint Florimond and Champignol)

Champignol I'll find you again. I'll find you.

Florimond Yes . . . In the meantime, I'm getting out of here.

(Saint Florimond runs out upstage right, between guard-room and canteen)

Champignol Catch him. Catch him.

Angele Robert!

Champignol Get out of my way.

All *(Surrounding Champignol)* Keep calm. Keep calm.

(From the moment the fight started, the dialogue is only just distinguishable above the general hubbub. Grosbon runs in from the guardroom and comes downstage to 3)

Grosbon Where is he? Where is he?

(Ledoux enters from the first hut)

Ledoux What's happening? What's all this noise about? What do you want, Corporal?

Grosbon Private Champignol, sir. He's escaped.

Ledoux Escaped?

Grosbon Yes, he broke the door down. *(To the Reservists)* Has anyone seen Champignol?

Champignol *(Advancing)* Champignol? What do you want with Champignol? What are you saying about Champignol? I am Champignol!

Grosbon You are? Well, back to the guardroom!

Champignol Me?

All The guardroom!

(General tumult. Champignol is dragged off, right)

CURTAIN

Act III

(Madame Rivolet's House. The same evening.
A small drawing-room, with a door in the back wall, leading into the hall. Downstage right, another door. Midstage, a door at an angle, leading into other reception rooms. Downstage left, a door leading into Madame Rivolet's room. Midstage, a table laid with glasses, etc., for the reception, placed at an angle. Behind the table, a door leading into the kitchen. A chandelier upstage.
When the curtain rises, the Prince of Valence, still in uniform, is mounted on a pair of steps, arranging the chandelier. The steps are placed in such a way that the chandelier masks his face and only his legs can be seen. Jerome stands between the steps and the table, watching him.
Celestin, in a dinner jacket, enters midstage right)

Celestin Jerome! Really! Jerome!

Jerome (*At 1*) Sir?

Celestin (*At 2*) What is going on?

Jerome (*Pointing to the Prince*) The orderly the Captain sent is arranging the chandelier.

Celestin Ah, good! Where are the drinks?

Jerome (*Passing behind the table, which he sets out during the following dialogue*) I'm getting them ready, sir.

Celestin (*Going to the table*) Well, hurry up. Everybody's asking for them.

(*Adrienne enters in evening dress, midstage right and comes downstage to 3, between the steps and the table*)

Adrienne Celestin! Do tell them to serve the drinks. Everyone's dying of thirst.

Celestin I was just telling Jerome.

(*Camaret, in tails, enters midstage right*)

Camaret Celestin! Aren't we getting anything to drink? Everybody's tongue's hanging out.

Celestin Yes, Uncle, I was just . . .

Camaret (*To Jerome, going towards the table and passing under the steps*) Well, hurry up, we're dying of thirst. (*When he gets under the steps, he stops*) Has that orderly arrived?

Jerome Yes, sir. He's arranging the chandelier. (*He points*)

Camaret (*Raising his head*) Ah! Good! Don't hesitate to use him for washing glasses . . . any odd jobs about the kitchen. (*To the Prince*) Eh, orderly?

The Prince (*On the steps*) Sir?

Camaret What's your name?

The Prince Prince of Valence.

Camaret Of course. Well, Prince of Valence, you'll stay in the kitchen, right? Under command of the butler.

The Prince Very good, sir. (*Aside*) Highly honoured!

Camaret You'll help wash the glasses. Do you know how to wash glasses?

The Prince (*Coming down the steps*) I regret I have never been taught to, sir.

Camaret Well, they'll show you. Run along.

The Prince What decadence!

(*The Prince goes out upstage, carrying the steps*)

Camaret (*To Jerome*) Come on. Take the drinks in.

Jerome Right, sir. (*He passes behind Camaret and goes towards the right with his tray*)

Camaret Hey, not so fast! (*Jerome stops at 4. Camaret takes a glass*) It's not like the Gospel here. The first . . . shall be first!

(*Jerome goes out, midstage right*)

Camaret (*To Celestin*) Phew! It's beginning to get hot in there.

Celestin (*Passing behind Adrienne to 2*) Well, the whole town's here.

Camaret Including that Saint Florimond of yours?

Celestin I must say he's not in much of a hurry for a suitor.

Adrienne (*Aside*) Does he want him to come?

Camaret Do you know this Saint Florimond?

Celestin No, nobody does, except Mother. And she can't get about. With her gout. So I'll have to introduce him. But I don't know what he looks like.

Camaret You'll recognise him . . . by his name! I'm going back into the cauldron. Call me, when he arrives.

Celestin Yes, Uncle.

(*Camaret goes out midstage right*)

Adrienne (*Downstage centre, aside*) To think he'll let me marry! . . . And will never know!

Celestin (*Going behind Adrienne to the table and pouring a glass of champagne*) Won't you join me, Adrienne? A little champagne?

Adrienne I'd love some. (*Celestin gives her a glass; she drinks a little*)

Celestin (*Watching her; aside*) How pretty she is!

Adrienne Why are you looking at me like that?

Celestin You know . . . I did admire you just now. It was wonderful the way you took your mother's place.

Adrienne (*Giving him her glass*) Oh, was that why?

Celestin (*Holding the glass*) You'd be a marvellous hostess!

Adrienne I'd better be, as I'm going to be married.

Celestin I'm sorry Monsieur de Saint Florimond wasn't here to see you.

Adrienne (*Offended*) Oh, you're sorry! He'll have time enough to find out, if I marry him.

Celestin Of course. Of course. (*Not knowing what to say, he puts Adrienne's glass to his lips, thinking it is his own*)

Adrienne (*Quickly*) That's my glass! I've just drunk from it.

Celestin Oh, I'm sorry. (*He puts it back on the table*)

Adrienne (*Offended*) That's something Monsieur de Saint Florimond would not have done.

Celestin What is?

Adrienne Not drink from a glass because my lips touched it.

Celestin Now look! *I* can't do anything right. But Monsieur de Saint Florimond . . . the so-called suitor . . . the so-called lover . . .

Adrienne But you're not in love. I suppose that's what you mean?

Celestin I mean I'm not your suitor.

Adrienne Precisely.

Celestin (*Aside, looking at her*) How pretty she is! (*Aloud*) You know, if you weren't my cousin, I would be your suitor.

Adrienne Then I'm sorry we're cousins.

Celestin You're laughing at me. Monsieur de Saint Florimond can be proud of having a wonderful wife. You can trust me to sing your praises.

Adrienne You're too kind.

Celestin Apparently he's a charming man.

Adrienne Oh!

Celestin Yes. He's rich – that doesn't matter, you are too – and he has a great name. You'll be the Countess de Saint Florimond. That sounds splendid. Countess de Saint Florimond.

Adrienne Yes, yes. That does sound splendid.

Celestin He's so distinguished and intelligent.

Adrienne (*Impatiently*) Oh, for heaven's sake, that's enough! You make me want to marry him right away!

Celestin If he's everything he's said to be, that wouldn't be so bad. Just think. A husband who's young, handsome, intelligent. He'll be so kind and loving . . .

Adrienne (*Tapping her foot*) Please, please! That's enough!

Celestin What's the matter?

Adrienne You do carry on about Monsieur de Saint Florimond's virtues. If you were a marriage broker you couldn't do better.

Celestin But Adrienne . . . What I said . . .

Adrienne What you said! I may become his wife! Does that mean nothing to you?

Celestin Well, you'll marry somebody some day.

Adrienne You're right. So it might as well be him as anyone else. As you're so insistent, I'll marry your Saint Florimond!

Celestin Adrienne, what is it? Are you angry?

Adrienne Oh Celestin, Celestin! I didn't expect this of you.

Celestin Great heavens! What's the matter with her? Adrienn

Adrienne (*In tears*) When we were children and promised to be husband and wife . . . was it only a game?

Celestin What! This can't be true!

Adrienne I thought it was in earnest. I've always said to myself: That's the man you must love, because he will be your husband.

Celestin Adrienne! Don't say another word. Unless you wan me to throw Saint Florimond out of the window as soon as he enters this house.

Adrienne Really? You'd do that for me?

Celestin Of course I would. Don't you realise I haven't forgotten either? You've been saying: That's the man I must love, because he'll be my husband. I've been saying: That's the girl I must not love, because she can't be my wife.

Adrienne Why?

Celestin Why? Because you're so rich . . .

Adrienne (*Joyfully*) Was that why? Oh, you're so stupid!

Celestin Yes, I am stupid . . . But that was why.

Adrienne Oh, it was . . . You're going to marry me immediately!

Celestin Me?

Adrienne Yes, you! And as you feel so guilty about it, I'll tell Father he can keep his sixty thousand francs a year. There!

Celestin You know, I think I can forget about your fortune.

Adrienne Now you are going to apologise.

Celestin Adrienne!

Adrienne No, not like that. (*Giving a military order*) Down on your knees!

Celestin (*Kneeling*) Very good, my commanding officer.

Adrienne (*Embracing him*) My husband.

(*Camaret enters midstage right*)

Camaret Well! I must say! What a way to carry on! What are you two up to?

Adrienne (*At 2*) Father!

(*Celestin quickly gets to his feet*)

Camaret (*At 3*) Don't let me disturb you. (*He passes behind Adrienne and stands between her and Celestin at 2*) Is this how you behave when you're about to meet a suitor? . . . But I'm sorry Monsieur de Saint Florimond isn't here.

Adrienne (*At 3*) Oh, Father! Monsieur de Saint Florimond doesn't matter any more. You said you'd never stand in the way of my true feelings. Well, the man I love and am going to marry . . . is here. (*She points to Celestin*)

Camaret (*Bursting out laughing*) Eh? Him? Extraordinary! This young rascal! Why . . . I've known him since he was so high.

Celestin I've grown since then, Uncle.

Camaret No, I'll never stand in the way of your true feelings. But, good God, why didn't you tell me sooner? You let your aunt hunt for suitors, organise a party . . .

Adrienne Never mind . . . It will be our engagement party.

Camaret Ah well . . . I like things to be done in a regular military manner . . . You love each other, you can get married.

Celestin Oh! Uncle!

Camaret Go on. Give her a kiss.

Adrienne That's what he was doing when you came in.

Camaret Carry on then. Last time it was illegal. Now it's official. (*He passes behind Adrienne and comes down to 3*)

Adrienne (*To Celestin*) Now . . . shun! (*She offers her cheek*)

Celestin (*Kissing her*) I preferred it when it was illegal.

(*A carriage is heard*)

Camaret Damn! That must be Saint Florimond.

Adrienne (*Quickly giving her arm to Celestin*) Saint Florimond!

Celestin Let's get out of here.

(*They run off right. Camaret follows them upstage to try to stop them and disappears for a moment. Jerome enters from the hall*)

Jerome Madame Champignol!

(*Angele enters, in evening dress, with a cloak, and comes downstage left. Jerome goes out*)

Angele I'm being very daring, but you can often escape danger by going to meet it.

(*Camaret enters midstage right*)

Captain!

Camaret Madame Champignol! It wasn't you I was expecting

Angele Who was it then?

Camaret Nobody important. A man who wants to marry my daughter.

Angele Oh!

Camaret Yes, no one you'd know. A Monsieur de Saint Florimond.

Angele Saint Florimond! (*Aside*) He hasn't arrived yet. It may still be all right.

Camaret It is kind of you to come, you gave me so little hope . . .

Angele I managed to postpone my return to Paris.

Camaret How very charming! Would you like to take off your . . . what's its name . . . greatcoat?

Angele My evening wrap.

Camaret Yes, I don't know the right name for that sort of thing.

(*Jerome enters from the hall*)

Ah, Jerome! Get . . . whoever's in charge of the stores.

Jerome In charge of the stores?

Camaret Yes. For the lady's wrap.

Jerome Oh, the woman in charge of the cloakroom! That's the maid, sir. You have to ring twice . . . (*He points to the bell, which is on the left of the door into the hall*)

Camaret Go on then, ring.

Jerome (*Going to the bell, ringing it and coming downstage to 3*) She doesn't know the house yet, sir. She only arrived this morning.

(*Jerome goes out, downstage right. Charlotte enters from the hall*)

Charlotte Did somebody ring for me?

Angele (*Aside*) Charlotte here!

Charlotte (*Coming downstage to 2*) Madame Champignol! What a surprise!

Camaret Ah! If I'm not mistaken . . . that's the maid you had in Paris.

Angele No . . . Yes. Yes. It is.

Charlotte Yes, Madame Champignol had the honour of having me as a maid.

Camaret All right, all right. Stop chattering. Come on, be off with it.

(*Angele takes off her cloak*)

Charlotte Very good, sir. (*She passes in front of Camaret and goes towards the door, downstage right*)

Camaret Where are you going?

Charlotte (*At 3*) Back to the cloakroom, sir. You said: Be off with you.

Camaret (*Aside*) The girl's an idiot. (*Aloud*) I said: Be off with *it*. The lady's wrap!

Charlotte (*Passing in front of Camaret towards Angele*) You should speak more clearly.

Angele (*At 1, giving her the cloak*) Here it is.

Camaret Be careful with it. (*Passing in front of Charlotte and going to Angele*) Now, if you will allow me to offer you my arm . . .

Angele (*Taking his arm*) Captain!

Camaret This way . . . (*As he passes in front of Charlotte*) Be careful you don't crease it.

(*Camaret and Angele go out midstage right*)

Charlotte (*Coming downstage*) Crease it! I wouldn't crease a beautiful coat like this. A wrap they call it! If I gave myself to a banker (*She puts her hand on her stomach*) I might carry the rap! Let's try it on. (*She does so*) It suits me.

(*The Prince enters downstage right, with a tray*)

The Prince (*Talking into the wings*) On the table? Right. (*Aside*) A lady!

Charlotte (*At 1, aside*) A soldier!

The Prince (*At 2, aside*) She must be one of the local aristocracy

Charlotte (*Laughing affectedly*) Ha ha ha!

The Prince (*Aside*) Is that for me? (*Laughing with embarrassment*) Ho ho ho! (*Aside*) This tray embarrasses me. (*Putting it under his arm*) I may be in uniform, but I'm not what you think I am.

Charlotte Would you like to know something? Me neither. I'm not what you think I am.

The Prince I am the Prince of Valence.

Charlotte Yes? I'm the maid.

The Prince The maid?

Charlotte (*Showing Angele's cloak*) I'm taking this to the cloakroom.

(*Camaret enters midstage right*)

Camaret (*Seeing Charlotte from behind*) A lady!

Charlotte The captain!

Camaret (*Passing behind the Prince towards Charlotte*) The maid! Make yourself at home. That's Madame Champignol's evening wrap.

Charlotte I'm giving it an airing. So it won't get creased.

Camaret Yes. All right. Go and put it away. As for you, Orderly, go back to the kitchen and don't let me catch you chasing after the maids again.

The Prince Me! Chase after maids! I don't chase after maids!

Camaret What did you say?

The Prince I said I don't chase after maids!

Camaret Shut up.

The Prince (*Going towards the door, downstage right*) All right! But I don't chase after maids!

Camaret I told you to shut up!

The Prince (*As he disappears*) All right! But I don't chase after maids!

(*The Prince goes out downstage right*)

Camaret What! I'll give you 'I don't chase after maids'! I'll teach you!

(*Camaret goes out, after the Prince*)

Charlotte That soldier's going to get into trouble.

(*Romeo enters from the hall, followed by Mauricette. He is in tails, she in evening dress*)

Romeo Come along, Mauricette.

Mauricette Yes, Father. (*She passes in front of him to 1*)

Romeo (*At 2*) Where's your husband?

Mauricette He's handing in our coats.

Romeo Ah, good. (*To Charlotte, who has remained upstage, folding Angele's cloak*) Where is Madame Rivolet? You see, she doesn't know us.

Charlotte In bed, sir. (*Voices off, right*) But here's her brother.

(*Charlotte goes out into the hall. Camaret enters downstage right*)

Camaret I'll wring that man's neck for him! I'll wring his neck!

Mauricette }
Romeo } The Captain!

Camaret (*Coming downstage to 3*) Madame Dufoulay! . . . Signor Romeo!

Mauricette (*Aside*) Heavens! My husband's meant to be under arrest.

Camaret What a delightful surprise!

Romeo Yes, Madame Rivolet was kind enough to ask us.

Mauricette I gather she's ill.

Camaret Yes, a bout of gout.

Romeo What a terrible business (*peessiness*)! What a terrible business!

Camaret I'm happy to welcome you in her place. I'm only sorry your husband couldn't come with you. But he's under arrest.

Mauricette Yes, yes, so he is. (*Aside*) Oh dear!

Romeo (*Passing in front of Mauricette to 1*) My son-in-law is going to enjoy himself!

(*Adrienne and Celestin enter right, laughing, arm in arm*)

Camaret What's the matter with you two young things?

Adrienne (*Coming downstage right*) We've been dancing madly. Oh! Madame Dufoulay and Signor Romeo!

Camaret (*At 3*) Let me introduce you to an engaged couple.

Romeo Oh!

Mauricette This is something new?

Camaret It's ten minutes old.

Mauricette (*Passing in front of Camaret to 3*) Congratulations!

Adrienne I told you I had an idea of my own. This is who it was.

Camaret Now, Celestin, give Madame Dufoulay your arm.

(*Celestin passes in front of Adrienne and offers his arm to Mauricette; together they go upstage right*)

Mauricette (*Aside*) Oh heavens! My husband's going to arrive!

Romeo Come, Mauricette . . .

(*Romeo goes out midstage right after Celestin and Mauricette*)

Adrienne Well, Father, aren't you coming in?

Camaret No, I can't stand ovens. There are too many people in there. There's no air left.

(*Jerome enters from the hall*)

Jerome Monsieur Dufoulay!

Camaret What!

(*Dufoulay enters in very new tails, putting on his gloves*)

Dufoulay Good evening. (*Coming downstage to 2 and finding himself face to face with Camaret*) The captain!

Camaret You!

Dufoulay (*Very embarrassed*) No. No.

Camaret What do you mean, no!

Dufoulay Hm! Yes. Yes.

Camaret What are you doing here? Why aren't you in the guardroom?

Dufoulay I . . . I . . .

Camaret What do you mean: I? What reason can you give me for coming to this ball?

Dufoulay Er . . . I didn't expect to find *you* here, Captain.

Camaret Is that why?

Dufoulay Yes. Yes.

Camaret Outrageous! Never mind. In this house you are our guest. Give my daughter your arm.

Dufoulay (*Giving Adrienne his arm*) Oh, Captain . . .

Camaret And when you get back to barracks tomorrow, add two days to your punishment.

Dufoulay What!

Camaret Be off with you.

Dufoulay (*Dumbfounded*) Very good, sir. (*To Adrienne as they go towards the door midstage right*) Delightful party this is . . .

(*Adrienne and Dufoulay go out*)

Camaret (*Going to the table*) Poor fellow, I must say it's bad luck finding me here. I have to be strict, though I've nothing against him. (*Drinking a glass of champagne*) I remember, before I was an officer, I was once confined to barracks. I went to a ball and had the same bad luck. I ran into my captain. He said: 'I know your face, aren't you in my company?' I replied: 'I'm Saint Florentin'. There wasn't any Saint Florentin in the company, but it went off as smoothly as posting a letter. Talking of Saint Florentin, Monsieur de Saint Florimond's still not arrived. But perhaps it's for the best, he's no reason to now.

(*Jerome enters from the hall*)

Jerome Monsieur de Saint Florimond!

Camaret Talk of the devil!

(*Saint Florimond enters, in tails*)

St Florimond (*Coming downstage to 2*) I'm a little late.

Camaret Monsieur Champignol!

St Florimond The Captain!

Camaret You! You here!

St Florimond No. No.

Camaret What do you mean, No. No! They all say No. No.

St Florimond Yes. Yes.

Camaret Has the whole battalion decided to come here?

St Florimond (*Aside*) Too bad, the scandal's broken. Her husband knows everything, I've no need to hide now. (*Aloud*) Captain, I am not Champignol.

Camaret (*Joking*) Well, well! Ha-ha! You aren't . . . Really! He's another of them! Who are you then, may I ask?

St Florimond You've just heard. I am Monsieur de Saint Florimond.

Camaret Saint Florimond! Oh, no. That's the limit. No. You're pretty impudent, I must say!

St Florimond I swear . . .

Camaret No, I tell you, no! I know that one. I invented it.

Florimond Invented what?

Camaret Yes, if you meet your captain, you give a false name. Yes. But to bring it off, the Captain mustn't know you as well as I do.

Florimond I can't explain, but I swear I am Saint Florimond.

Camaret Now, look. I've been to your studio. I've had you in my regiment, you started my portrait. And now you're trying to make me believe you're not Champignol, the painter Champignol, the reservist in my company.

Florimond I am not Champignol.

Camaret But you are Saint Florimond.

Florimond (*Passing to 1*) Exactly.

Camaret My dear fellow, you've no luck with the name you've chosen. You thought you'd picked one out of the air. Well, Saint Florimond exists and we're expecting him this evening. That's a shock for you, eh?

Florimond No.

Camaret He's coming here to marry my daughter.

Florimond (*Aside*) She's his daughter!

Camaret Though he's on a wild goose chase. She's engaged already.

Florimond Engaged!

Camaret Well, what have you to say to that, eh?

Florimond I have to say there's been a mistake. I am Saint Florimond, I am not Champignol. If you have a Champignol in your company, he's still there.

Camaret (*Aside*) Really! There can't be two men as alike as this. Though . . . twins . . . (*Aloud*) Right, I'll confirm what you say. (*He goes to the door, midstage right*)

Florimond What's he going to do?

Camaret Orderly!

(The Prince enters midstage right and remains in the doorway)

The Prince (*Saluting, then noticing Saint Florimond*) Champignol!

Camaret (*At 2*) There! You see! I didn't make him say it. Orderly, run back to barracks and tell them to send along Private Champignol, now under arrest.

St Florimond What!

The Prince (*Dumbfounded*) Private Champignol!

Camaret Yes. I understand your surprise, but do as I say.

The Prince Very good, sir. (*Aside, going towards the door*) The captain's going mad . . . mad!

(The Prince goes out into the hall)

Camaret Now we shall learn the truth.

St Florimond Yes. (*Aside*) Ohhh! They're going to bring the husband here!

Camaret Do you still insist you're not Champignol?

St Florimond Definitely.

(Charlotte enters upstage right, with a tray)

Charlotte Oh! Monsieur Champignol!

Camaret Look. Look. Your own maid!

St Florimond (*At 1*) Ha, the maid! What does a maid know?

Charlotte (*Passing in front of Camaret to 2*) How are you, Monsieur Champignol?

St Florimond (*Pushing her away to 1*) Go away.

(Charlotte goes out into the hall. Dufoulay and Mauricette enter downstage right)

Dufoulay Hullo! Champignol!

Mauricette Monsieur Champignol!

Camaret The family too! Do you disown your family?

St Florimond Ohhh!

(Romeo enters downstage right)

Romeo Hullo! Champignol!

Camaret There!

Romeo (*Coming downstage to 3*) How are you?

St Florimond Oh, go to hell.

Romeo What's the matter with him?

Camaret He's trying to make me believe he's not Champignol.

Romeo (*Laughing, passing to 2*) That's marvellous. Clever, eh? Because you're under arrest!

Florimond (*Furious*) I told you to shut up.

Romeo Pah!

(*Angele enters midstage right*)

Camaret Ah! Here's a witness who'll be more convincing than any of them.

Angele (*Aside*) Saint Florimond . . . Here!

Camaret (*To Angele*) You can help us. (*Pointing to Saint Florimond*) Who is this man?

Angele (*At 4*) Why . . . it's Monsieur Champignol, my husband.

Camaret Ah! There!

Florimond Her as well!

Camaret For the last hour he's been insisting he's Monsieur de Saint Florimond.

Angele Really? How awful! He's had another attack.

All Attack?

Florimond What does she mean, attack?

Angele Oh, Captain, if you only knew! Every now and then his mind wanders; he thinks he's someone else.

Florimond Eh? What's she saying?

Angele Only the other day . . . He thought he was President . . . he kept on making speeches.

Florimond Me?

Romeo Yes, that does happen. I once heard about a man who always stood like this. (*He puts his left hand on his hip, with his right arm stretched out horizontally, the hand gently curved downwards*)

All Why?

Romeo He thought he was a teapot.

Angele There you are! Exactly the same! Oh, dear! Oh, dear!

St Florimond (*Aside*) They're trying to get me certified. Certified

Camaret Yes, this is serious. Would you like me to send for the MO?

Angele You needn't worry. It never lasts long.

St Florimond (*Furiously striding up and down in front of the others, who retreat terrified upstage, forming a semicircle*) Attacks! I don't have attacks! It's all a joke!

All Yes, yes, a joke!

St Florimond (*Back to the audience*) But it is a joke! It is! I told you I am Saint Florimond.

All Yes, yes, you are Saint Florimond.

St Florimond (*Coming downstage to the left, at 1*) Oh, they're getting on my nerves!

Camaret (*To Angele*) If only I'd thought of you earlier, I needn't have sent an orderly back to barracks to get the real Champignol.

Angele (*Aside, leaving the group upstage and coming down to 2*) They're bringing my husband here!

Camaret (*Coming down to 3*) We'll leave you alone with Monsieur Champignol. In this situation a wife can do more good than strangers.

Angele I'm very grateful.

Romeo (*Who has remained upstage with Mauricette and Dufoulay*) Come along.

Mauricette Poor Monsieur Champignol!

Romeo What a terrible business!

(*They all go out except Angele and Saint Florimond*)

St Florimond They're driving me mad!

Angele Look what you've done. It's your fault they've gone to get my husband.

St Florimond Thank heavens! Let him come. It's time someone put an end to this outrageous situation I've been floundering in for the last twenty-four hours.

Angele Then you're going to ruin me? You want a scandal

St Florimond If there's any scandal, it's your husband's fault.

I'd have done anything to avoid it. Now he knows everything and is shouting it all over the rooftops, why should I go on playing this ridiculous part?

Angele What's going to happen to me? What do I become? A dishonoured woman, rejected by my husband! Your mistress, which I've never been! All because of you!

Florimond (*Passing to 2*) Ah well, Angele! It's fate.

Angele (*At 1*) Fate! You mean your clumsiness. But you don't care. When my husband kills you, you won't give a thought to me.

Florimond What! Kill me?

Angele Don't you deserve it?

(*The Prince enters from the hall*)

The Prince (*Talking into the wings*) Come on, Champignol. Come on in.

Florimond He's coming! Let's get out of here.

(*Saint Florimond runs out downstage right*)

Angele That's typical. He runs away.

(*Champignol enters upstage*)

The Prince Stay here. I'll tell the Captain.

(*The Prince goes out midstage right*)

Angele My husband! Well, it's for the best.

Champignol (*Coming downstage to 2*) Angele! . . . Darling! . . . You, Madame!

Angele (*At 1*) Robert . . . Let me explain . . .

Champignol Stand back. (*Passing to 1*) This is the woman I married! Not only did I marry her, I gave her my name! She was a Chapouillet, I made her a Champignol!

Angele Robert, don't be angry with me.

Champignol (*Passing behind Angele and coming downstage to 2*) I'm appalled! Appalled!

Angele Robert . . .

Champignol (*Going upstage and furiously throwing his cap on the ground*) No! When I think about it, my hair stands on end.

Angele (*At 1*) Appearances are against me, but I'm not guilty.

Champignol Nonsense! You're not going to tell me he's not your lover!

Angele Who?

Champignol Augustus.

Angele Augustus?

Champignol Augustus. The natural son of the Roman Emperor

Angele What?

Champignol He's doing Potard's service for him. You know Potard. That's him!

Angele What's he saying?

Champignol (*Tearing his hair, which he hasn't got*) Oh, I'm appalled! Appalled!

Angele Robert, you must be confused. You mean Monsieu de Saint Florimond.

Champignol Saint Florimond? He told me Augustus. Never mind. Do you dare to say he's not your lover?

Angele My lover? Never.

Champignol Nonsense! He admitted it.

Angele It isn't true.

Champignol He said: 'There's never been anything between this woman and me'. Never! Do you hear?

Angele Exactly. Well?

Champignol Exactly. You're not going to tell me that if a man says that about a woman, there never has been anything between them!

Angele What's he to say when it's true?

Champignol (*Taken aback*) That's right.

Angele Robert, let me explain.

Champignol (*Dramatically*) Very well, then!

Angele Everything I've done was for your sake.

Champignol Nonsense! For my . . . I never expected that!

Angele It was for you. There has never been anything between Monsieur de Saint Florimond and me. I swear it . . . on your head.

Champignol No, please . . . leave my head alone.

Angele All right. On my mother's head.

Champignol That's better. On my mother-in-law's head.

Angele You were away and he was pursuing me. He was there when the police came to arrest you as a deserter. So I thought I'd teach him a lesson he won't forget. I said to the police: 'You're looking for Monsieur Champignol. Here he is.'

Champignol What! Is that true?

Angele I did it for the honour of your name.

Champignol (*Laughing*) For the honour . . . What a joke! What a joke!

Angele That's why he was brought here instead of you.

Champignol Now I understand. What a joke! I'm delighted. Delighted!

Angele Well, are you satisfied?

Champignol Yes, I am. Mademoiselle Chapouillet, you are worthy of the name of Champignol.

Angele (*Rushing into his arms*) Robert! . . . What are we going to do?

Champignol What?

Angele The Captain's convinced Saint Florimond is Champignol.

Champignol He is, is he? Don't worry. I've an idea . . .

Angele But . . .

Champignol Yes, yes. I'm going to get my own back on Saint Florimond. Augustus!

Angele (*At 1*) Here he is.

(*Camaret enters midstage right with Saint Florimond and the others*)

Camaret They've found Champignol in barracks?

Florimond I told you, Captain . . .

Camaret (*Seeing Champignol and coming downstage to 3*) This man! Nonsense, you're quite different! (*To everybody*) You all know him, is he Champignol?

All No. No.

St Florimond Yes! All right, ask him.

Camaret (*To Champignol*) Come here. What's your name?

Champignol (*Aside*) You wait! You wait, Augustus! (*Aloud*) My name is Saint Florimond.

St Florimond (*Dumbfounded*) What!

Camaret There! I knew it!

St Florimond This is too much. *I* am!

Camaret Not again!

Angele It's another attack, Captain. (*She goes upstage with Camaret*)

All (*Also going upstage*) Another attack!

(*During the following two lines, Angele, Camaret and Romeo talk quietly together upstage. Dufoulay and Mauricette pass behind them and come downstage to 1 and 2*)

St Florimond (*Whispering to Champignol*) You dare to say . . .

Champignol (*Sharply*) Exactly. And I forbid you to deny it, Augustus!

Camaret (*Coming downstage between Champignol and Saint Florimond. To Saint Florimond*) Well, are you better now? Do you still maintain you're Saint Florimond

Florimond You're right, Captain, I am Champignol.

Camaret (*Triumphant*) There! You see!

Angele (*Pretending to be overjoyed and coming downstage to 3*) His attack's over at last.

(*Romeo comes down to 7*)

Camaret (*To Champignol*) Oh! . . . Saint Florimond, Saint Florimond! Extraordinary! I haven't got a Saint Florimond in my company.

Champignol The fact is I'm not a soldier. This uniform was lent to me, because I fell in the river.

Romeo What!

Camaret He did too.

hampignol I was fishing from the bank.

Romeo You didn't try to jump onto a tree stump that was covered with mud?

hampignol Exactly. And splash! I fell in.

Romeo You'll never believe it, but exactly the same thing happened to me.

hampignol Really?

Romeo Word of honour!

Camaret I'll have to do something about that tree stump.

(*Adrienne enters downstage right with Celestin*)

Adrienne What are you all plotting about?

Camaret Ah! Good! Here's Adrienne.

(*Adrienne comes downstage to 7, Celestin to 8*)

(*Pointing to Champignol*) Let me introduce Monsieur de Saint Florimond.

Adrienne (*Aside*) They wanted me to marry him! He's bald!

Camaret My dear Monsieur de Saint Florimond, I'm sorry to tell you my daughter is engaged to her cousin Celestin.

hampignol Never mind, Captain, I'm delighted to hear it.

Camaret Oh! Ah, he's making the best of it. (*To Saint Florimond*) As for you, Champignol, get back to barracks.

Florimond (*Aside*) So I've got to take his place for the next month. It's the last time I'll get caught pursuing married women.

Camaret And don't let me have to tell you again. Your hair's too long. Get it cut.

hampignol Yes, give him a close shave. That's what I've had.

CURTAIN